DEMCO

LEARNING DISABILITY

LEARNING DISABILITY
The Imaginary Disease

THOMAS G. FINLAN

Foreword by Michael R. Valentine

BERGIN & GARVEY
Westport, Connecticut • London

Library of Congress Cataloging-in-Publication Data

Finlan, Thomas G.
    Learning disability : the imaginary disease / Thomas G. Finlan :
foreword by Michael R. Valentine.
      p. cm.
    Includes bibliographical references and index.
    ISBN 0-89789-345-X (alk. paper).—ISBN 0-89789-351-4 (pbk.)
    1. Learning disabled children. 2. Learning disabled children—
Education. 3. Learning disabled children—Identification.
    I. Title.
    LC4704.F55   1994
    371.9—dc20   93-18136

British Library Cataloguing in Publication Data is available.

Library of Congress Catalog Card Number: 93-18136
ISBN: 0-89789-345-X
      0-89789-351-4 (pbk.)

First published in 1994

Bergin & Garvey, 88 Post Road West, Westport, CT 06881
An imprint of Greenwood Publishing Group, Inc.

Printed in the United States of America

The paper used in this book complies with the
Permanent Paper Standard issued by the National
Information Standards Organization (Z39.48-1984).

10 9 8 7 6 5 4 3 2 1

Copyright Acknowledgment

The author and the publisher are grateful to the following for
granting the use of material:

Ann Landers column of August 21, 1992. Permission granted by
Ann Landers and Creators Syndicate.

This book is dedicated to my mother,
Myrtle Finlan, who taught me that
teaching is the most noble of all professions.

Contents

Foreword

In one of my books, I used the drawing below to illustrate a fundamental point—that based on how you define things, or the words you use to describe those things—the process of labeling alone will actually help create your perceptions of reality and the way you see the world.

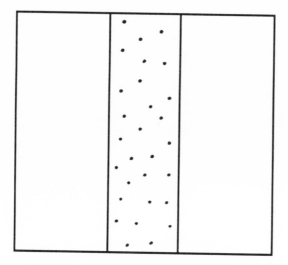

This simple drawing is presented so you can see how your perceptions of this drawing change as the words or labels used to describe the drawing change. First, however, please look at the drawing for a minute or two and let your imagination go. What do you think it could be? What does the drawing represent? What is reality? Look at it for a while before proceeding.

Is it a picture of flies stuck to a Shell Pest-Strip? A window with curtains half open, revealing snowflakes or rain outside? Germs under a microscope? People seen from the top of the Empire State Building? A partially open observatory dome showing the stars?

From what I understand, this picture is actually a drawing in a museum entitled, "A giraffe passing a second-story window."

Although the lines of the drawing never change, one begins to perceive them differently once a word, a label, a trait, a concept, or a belief is attached. In response to the suggestion that the drawing is a giraffe's neck passing a second-story window, one sees it as a giraffe. One begins to see it, to believe it, and to react and feel toward it as if it were really a giraffe.

This fundamental principle of the words used to define a concept having profound effects on the way the world is seen is one of the critical problems in education in general, and the whole area of learning disabilities, as well as the concept of attention deficit/hyperactivity disorder, specifically.

Today there are two major conceptual ways to see the social evils of schools, as well as the world. One is to try to explain problems from a social, cultural, psychological, educational, training, or learning perspective and the other is to try to explain these problems from a biochemical, neurological, medical model. Both of these ways of conceptualizing the world have profound effects on the way you see problems and the way you will intervene to try to solve those problems.

In the past thirty to forty years the medical model method of perceiving the world has infiltrated educational institutions. Within two to three decades this perception has created a delusional reality that millions of American children, mainly males, are biochemically imbalanced, neurologically defective, genetically flawed rejects, and, in some shape or form, handicapped.

In Dr. Finlan's book, he challenges us to question and analyze some of the underlying assumptions that the medical model uses to try to explain learning disabilities, and urges us to return to more parsimonious, pragmatic and effective solutions to children's school difficulties: effective parenting, disciplining, education, instructions, and training.

                                                 —Michael R. Valentine

1

LD Means Lousy Diagnosis

We are never deceived; we deceive ourselves.
Goethe

There is no such thing as a learning disability.

You may think LD exists since more than two million school children have currently been identified with this federally legislated disability, but LD does not exist any more than there are witches in Salem, monsters in Loch Ness, or abominable snowmen in the Himalayas. LD is a movement based on supposition, analogy, and guesswork. There never has been any scientific evidence that LD exists or any evidence that LD programs help students. Instead, LD theory and practices keep changing to accommodate current research most of which contradicts previous LD guesswork. Why does LD persist? Is there some conspiracy to hide the truth, to keep children in those classes down the hall, to deny them their right to a regular education? Of course not. There doesn't have to be a conspiracy. The control of LD was turned over to a bureaucracy so large and distant that no one is in charge. As the old saying goes, if you want to keep something from getting done, turn it over to a committee; and in the case of children's education, turn it over to the greatest bureaucracy in the world, the U.S. government.

WHAT IF THERE IS NO SUCH THING
AS LEARNING DISABILITIES?

Even though I am convinced there is no such thing as LD, you may see LD as an established fact. If so, ask yourself, "What if there is no such thing as learning disabilities?" instead of the more common question, "What *are* learning disabilities?" You might be forced to look at learning disabilities differently. A different perspective may get us out of our current misguided notions about LD. Answering the question (What if there is no such thing as learning disabilities?) may teach us quite a bit. Perhaps we would react differently to children who have difficulty in school, for our beliefs about LD cause us to view students in limiting ways. Changing our beliefs should change how we treat those students.

LD—PERMANENT, PERVASIVE, AND PERSONAL?

If you believe that UFOs exist, you might maintain that wearing aluminum foil under your clothing will shield you from their gamma rays. By the same token, if you believe LD exists, you might see those children as being "wired up wrong," as having a medical disability, a disease, a short circuit in the brain. You might believe that their problems were inherited, caused by a birth trauma, poor diet, eating red food dye, a high fever, or perhaps by poor life experiences during some critical period of development. Regardless, you would see the problem as a disability, a weakness, a deficiency that is somehow permanent, pervasive, and a characteristic of the child—personal in nature. That is the belief system of learning disabilities. Based on that belief system, you would treat any child so labeled in certain ways. For instance, your expectations regarding the student's ability to read and write, to sit still, to follow directions, or to tell time would be seriously diminished. Someone who is disabled is not able to do certain things. It would be cruel to try to get a crippled person to walk when he cannot. And, it would be cruel to expect an LD youngster to read, to cipher, or to sit still if you believe she cannot do those things, cannot help herself, and is the product of some predestined force.

On the other hand, if you were to suspend your beliefs about LD for a while and allow yourself to open up to other explanations—explanations that say LD is a myth, that children really are capable of the things we say they cannot do—perhaps you would expect more from that same youngster. If you believed that LD was a terrible hoax perpetrated on the youth of America—that, except for the most severely afflicted, all children are capable of learning to read, capable of sitting still, and capable of following directions—your expectations would change and so might the child's achievement. It is certainly an interesting thought.

IS LD A MYTH?

Is it possible that LD is a myth? That children so labeled are harmed by lowered expectations? That they act to fulfill those lowered expectations? That their disability is a result of the school system treating them improperly? The answers to those questions might help us change our thinking about LD, for if there is no LD—if LD is a terrible hoax—we have done irreparable harm to millions of already labeled youngsters. My hope is that you will, at least for the time that you are reading this book, suspend your beliefs about LD, that you will not think there is agreement among experts regarding LD theory (for there is no such agreement), that you will realize that LD theory is just that—theory—theory which has yet to be confirmed in any scientific investigation. I hope you will allow me to change your thinking. It is up to you.

You may continue to think that LD children or their backgrounds are at fault, that they are wired up wrong, that they will always have difficulty learning to read, sitting still, or following directions. You may lower your expectations and give them watered-down educational experiences, or you may decide that there are other explanations that are more kid-centered, that allow for explanations which do not blame the child, that see LD as a well-intentioned but misguided excursion into theoretical musings based on analogy. There truly are other explanations— explanations that allow children who seem to have difficulty in school to flourish.

ALL CHILDREN ARE CAPABLE

This book offers hope. Suspend your beliefs. Don't fall victim to the current thinking, for when adults hold the belief that certain children are not capable of learning, children are forced down the road of learned helplessness from which there is little hope of escape. In the United States, we have condemned millions of children to just such futures and continue to do so at a rate of nearly 200,000 more students each year. Instead of thinking that children are not capable of learning relatively simple tasks, think that LD is a myth and that children are capable of doing all that we have said they are not capable of doing. The expectations of the adults in the children's lives shape the children's achievement. Consider the following: "If changing beliefs would change children's performance, if LD theory really is wrong, would you want to continue to perpetrate such a terrible lie on America's youth?" I hope your answer is a resounding no.

This book offers a kinder, gentler explanation of LD. All children are created with a wondrous sense of curiosity and are programmed to learn at birth. The amount and types of learning that they engage in before school are far more intricate and involved than anything we ask of them in school. Childhood was designed for learning. It has been estimated that by the time children are three they have learned 60 percent of all that they will ever learn. Other species obtain adulthood in very short periods. With humans it takes time. Children are wonders and wondrous. They learn to walk, to talk, to control their sphincter muscles, to drink from a glass, to engage in intricate social situations, and to perform thousands of other complex behaviors without much, if any direct instruction. Why should we view those very same children as broken or diseased when they reach school age and cannot crack a simple code that was taught to them in esoteric and hidden ways? The notion that children are at fault for not learning to read is preposterous. Children are marvels who can learn to read, to write, and to cipher if they have not been too damaged by the trappings of labels and poor institutional practices. Education works. Children can learn. Forget all that nonsense about LD. LD is imaginary.

2

LD—The Imaginary Disease

Castles in the air are all right
until we try to move into them.
Author unknown

I attended a performance of Moliere's *The Imaginary Invalid* more than twenty-five years ago, about the time LD was getting its start. Although I remember little of the play, I vividly recall that the central character was a hypochondriac who desired (and enjoyed, in a perverse fashion) any medical attention which, in the seventeenth century, consisted principally of bleedings, purgatives, and enemas. The medical community of that time was composed of fakes and quacks who masked their lack of medical skill by use of Latin terms and by hiding behind a particular training not open to the average person.

I remember one of the doctors in *The Imaginary Invalid* running around the stage shouting instructions to a nurse, "Give-a-mum an enemum! Fix-a-mum a bleed-a-mum!"—those being the medical interventions of the time. The Latin terminology was used to disguise the doctor's lack of knowledge as to what to do. The doctor's actions from a twentieth-century point of view are laughable, but not if viewed in the light of seventeenth century medical beliefs and practices. People in Moliere's time sought just such medical treatment. In the final analysis, people who sought no medical treatment were probably better off than those who sought treatment because the medicine of Moliere's time was invasive, without scientific evidence of benefit, and perhaps downright harmful—much like the LD interventions of today. In Moliere's time, doctors spoke of enemas, purgatives, and bleedings. Today's LD practitioners speak of dyspraxia, hyperkinesis, attention deficit disorder, neuropsychological impairment, and the like using their own brand of Latin terminology. Moliere's hypochondriac was comforted when the doctor took action, regardless of how ill-suited it was. Naive parents today are mistakenly comforted when the statement, "Johnny can't read" is mysteriously transformed into the diagnosis, "Johnny has dyslexia," and when Johnny is transferred down the hall to a teacher who is overburdened with other children who cannot read just like Johnny.

THE TYPICAL LD CLASSROOM

In the United States, the typical LD teacher has an average of twenty-one children from three to six different grade levels who may need help in reading, writing, spelling, mathematics, science, social studies, note taking, study skills, and following directions. Not even the most gifted of teachers can provide meaningful instruction to twenty-one difficult-to-teach children in all of those subjects, even if the children are moved in and out of the classroom like cars on an assembly line.

Can you imagine planning lessons for children in fourth, fifth, and sixth grades who are reading two or more grade levels below placement—not just planning reading lessons—but spelling lessons, writing lessons, lessons in note taking, lessons in following directions; lessons in fourth-grade science, social studies, and health; in fifth-grade science, social studies, and health; in sixth-grade science, social studies, and health? The task is overwhelming. What usually happens is that the teacher does the best she can in grouping students and dividing her time. Most of the students get less instruction than they would have received if they had just stayed where they were. The treatment, because of the dilution of the teacher's time, becomes more harmful than leaving the students alone. Even more disturbing is the fact that the regular teacher has many others in her classroom with similar problems who cannot be distinguished in any concrete and consistent way from those selected to go to the LD room.

LD practice, as it currently exists, involves "enemums" with no sound measure of benefit administered to millions of children, most of whom cannot be distinguished from the rest of the school population. Despite that, children are segregated from their peers for all or part of the day; they are labeled with scientific and legal terms that seem somehow correct; and they, or the adults in their lives, become a party to the conspiracy. The interventions are jargoned, impressive sounding substitutes for proper care. The imaginary diseases are nouns and imply having something. He has a learning disability, much like one has a cold or the flu. But the symptoms he has are relative, not specific, a matter of degree, not absolute. The reasoning is circular. The diagnosis leads to the label which becomes the explanation. "Johnny cannot read; therefore, he is LD," almost magically becomes, "Johnny is LD; therefore, he cannot read."

It could be argued that the label would mean little if the interventions worked, if we could patch the children up and send them back to regular classes. Just as the medical practice of bleeding in the seventeenth century would not have been abandoned if it had worked, calling a child disabled would be okay if we could help after we labeled. But that is not the case.

LD IS A MADE-UP CATEGORY

LD is not some scientifically proven, hard-to-identify disease but a *made-up* category in which to place children. LD is just one of a number of labels current society applies to children's unacceptable behaviors. Delinquent, emotionally disturbed, incorrigible, disordered, at-risk, behaviorally impaired are some others. In the current manner in which we think of children, behaviors become symptoms, and in circular fashion, symptoms become disease. Children are not viewed as being capable, but are seen as victims of predestined forces.

We all know that we can define, organize, and arrange things in all sorts of fashions depending upon our needs. In fact, that is what language is for—to define, organize, and arrange. Learning disabilities theory is a product of language. It is a concept that was invented to help explain underachievement by children who seem bright enough not to be underachievers. The LD label is a device that helps us arrange and view children in a certain fashion. The definer selects the system and uses it for her own purposes, but it is an invention by human minds and does not exist outside of the creation. If the invention were helpful, it should be used. But the label does not help, the programs do not work, and we are harming our most precious natural resources, our children.

Most categories of the social sciences, just like LD, are not dichotomous, but are continuous. Hyperactivity, for example, is relative. How fidgety must someone be to be called hyperactive? The answer is always, "It depends." It depends on who is doing the determining and why. The problem is that most educational categories, like hyperactivity or attention deficit disorder, seem like they are dichotomous, and we treat them as such. For example, while I was a school psychologist, I met with some parents regarding their son's giftedness. I told them giftedness was merely a matter of degree, just like being tall. Some people are taller than others, and some people score higher on IQ tests than others. The father interrupted and asked if I was sure. He thought that being gifted was just like being pregnant—either you are or you are not. That is the deception of categories.

Of course, many categories are dichotomous by nature like the categories of *chair* or *organic substances*. Anything that cannot be identified as a chair is by definition a *non chair*. Sometimes it may be difficult to determine whether an object is a chair since a chair may not look like a chair. It may look more like a stool, and we may have difficulty classifying it, but it still is for sitting. By the same token, the presence of carbon determines whether something is *organic*. If there is no carbon, it is *nonorganic*.

How a human learns is far more fleeting than the properties of a chair or of organic material. The so-called symptoms of LD do not remain stable; they come and go with the wind. Classifying a child as handicapped based on something so fleeting as the inability to distinguish *no* from *on* is pure folly. A child who cannot distinguish *no* from *on* (or any of the myriad other behaviors that are symptoms of LD) can be taught that skill and then can no longer be disabled by that criterion. A chair will always be for sitting, but LD symptoms will fade.

LD is a category invented for convenience, just like shortness or kindness or mean-spiritedness are labels of convenience, and like all labels, existence depends on its acceptance by others. LD, as a category used to classify children, will exist only as long as people wish it to. When people agree that it no longer exists (or at least Congress agrees), it will no longer exist. My hope is to speed its demise.

LD: A MOVEMENT RUN AMOK

This book presents a clear-cut argument—that LD was a well-intentioned but ill-conceived movement that has run amok and is placing millions of youngsters on a disabling trajectory toward failure and low self-esteem from which there is little hope of escape. Some do escape, but they are few and they may carry the scars of mistaken beliefs with them the rest of their lives. I take one unequivocal stand—*The consequences of the label are so severe, and the children labeled are so harmed that we must end this category quickly and forever.* Labeling children as LD and shuttling them off to a down-the-hall existence is wrong. It sets up negative expectations for millions of youth and condemns them to the self-fulfilling consequences of that label. They are no longer expected to learn. Misbehavior is excused. They are segregated and set apart. The adults in their lives believe the children are less than whole and need excuses instead of instruction. The growth of LD has to do with social forces, politics, beliefs, and supposing, rather than science.

The beliefs and supposing about LD are centered around the incorrect notion that symptom equals disease. Just as a runny nose may mean many things, so too, may the inability to distinguish *b* from *d* mean many things. But for some reason, perhaps an inclination not to trust our own notions and the overwhelming attempt to "scientificize" data, people are afraid to speak up.

LD was originally conceived as minimal brain dysfunction. In effect, this meant that some children's brains were not working properly when it came to school work; but the dysfunctioning was so minimal that it could not be seen directly. That was the basic theory of LD presented in the 1960s and the impetus behind the acceptance of LD as a handicap in federal legislation. The legislation turned the control over to a bureaucracy that benefits greatly by perpetuating the myth. The hard facts are that the original theory of LD has passed from favor because there has been no evidence to push it beyond its theoretical musings. Instead, virtually all LD experts have come to think of LD as a pattern of symptoms (except for a very few, obviously brain-damaged students). Like a menu at a Chinese restaurant, taking one symptom here, one there, and depending upon the professionals doing the choosing, nearly any student can be labeled as LD. The original LD theory is gone, but the public has never been informed of the change in LD theorizing. They still see LD as faulty wiring. The monolithic bureaucracy of education has kept the myth intact.

MY DOUBTS ABOUT LD

I began my training as a school psychologist in 1974 when LD was gaining favor. I was beset with doubts. I have struggled with the concept of LD since that time. This book is based on my struggles with the concept of LD and the conclusions I have reached concerning it. For a long time, I was confused by the jargon and immobilized by my naivety, but eventually I came to one inescapable conclusion—*There is no such thing as LD.* It does not exist, and we are doing irreparable harm by placing children so-labeled into special education categories. For a long time, I have wanted to shout, "Stop doing that to our kids!" Then I feared no one would listen, but now I can be quiet no longer. Even if we had left the LD children to the devices of the regular education teachers to cope with them as they always have in the past—as slow learners—not as children who are wired up wrong and thus not responsible for their own learning, we would harm them less, but that is not what I am advocating. There is hope beyond that. We can help. Proper instruction is the real answer.

LD MEANS "LITTLE DUMMIES"

This book is about my conclusions: The labeling of children as LD is harmful. The programs do not work. We cannot even decide who should be labeled. The LD experience treats children as if they are dumb. They feel that they are inadequate and are unable to learn what their peers learn. Advocates can pretend all they like to the contrary, but, as one seven-year-old student told me, LD means "little dummies." He was more perceptive than most of the adults in his world. The conclusion is inescapable—we believe that LD children do not measure up.

Lest you think I am alone in my conclusions about LD, allow me to list a few comments that others have made. Peter Schrag and Diane Divoky have called LD "the invention of a disease,"[1] Bob Algozzine and Jim Ysseldyke have called LD "the oversophistication of a concept,"[2] Thomas McKnight has called LD "a myth."[3] Regarding LD inquiry, one researcher concluded that "The explorations have been minimal and the discoveries have been painfully sparse."[4] Scott Sigmon argues that the growth in the number of mildly handicapped children indicates two significant points:

(a) the increasing practice of labeling children as impaired learners is an attempt to preserve the rigid K-12 system and (b) stating that most of these impaired students have mild learning disabilities is a form of pneumatology (a ludicrous study of spirits applied to education).[5]

Another educator stated:

The child who is truly reading disabled (dyslexic) is very rare. When children are taught to read in a structured, teacher directed instructional program, they read. When this is not done, many children experience difficulty and are then mislabeled as dyslexic, an excuse.[6]

You can ignore what each of those experts has said, for there are many other experts who believe wholeheartedly in LD, but you may be excusing the poor achievement of students and perpetuating a system designed for failure.

THE OPINIONS EXPRESSED ARE MY OWN

A few years ago during a meeting at our office, I was expressing an opinion about a since forgotten topic when a truculent colleague interrupted me with, "That is *your* opinion!" I responded, "Of course, it is my opinion. I am the one talking." Well, this book expresses my opinions, too, since I am the one who is talking. This is not a research book and is not highly documented. It is opinion, but so is LD theory. This book is about why I believe that the concept of learning disabilities is wrong; that there is no evidence that confirms any of the suppositions regarding LD; and that there is no evidence to suggest that our methods of educating so-called LD children are helpful. In fact, quite the opposite is true. The application of the theories regarding LD is harmful no matter how well-intentioned.

This book is written for parents, educators, and others concerned with the quality of American education. I give examples from my own experiences and talk about things that are easy to recognize at nearly every school in America. I describe where LD came from, what is wrong with current LD explanations, and what you can do about them in your child's life, especially what to do if you accept my explanations. The answer as to what to do is simple. Stop believing in LD. Don't believe the so-called experts who want to label and segregate. Don't let anyone ever put a label on your child or you. You are the only one who can stop it. This book tells you how.

NOTES

1. Schrag, P., & Divoky, D. (1975). *The myth of the hyperactive child*. New York: Dell, p. 42.

2. Algozzine, B., & Ysseldyke, J. E. (1983). Learning disabilities as a subset of school failure: The oversophistication of a concept. *Exceptional Children*, 50(3), p. 242.

3. McKnight, R. T. (1982). The learning disability myth in American education. *Journal of Education*, 164(4), p. 351.

4. Barsch, R. (1986). A plea for a new direction. *Academic Therapy*, 22(1), p. 9.

5. Sigmon, S. B. (1990). *Critical voices on special education*. Albany: State University of New York Press, p. 1.

6. Burkhardt, M. (1981). In *Why Johnny still can't read*. R. Flesch (author). New York: Harper, p. xx.

3

A Smoke Screen of Precision

The worst deluded are the self deluded.
C. N. Bovee

In Pennsylvania, as in most states, the school psychologist is the gate-keeper of special education. Armed with a battery of tests, the school psychologist evaluates and pronounces judgments on children's abilities. Although recent laws have minimized the role psychologists play in labeling children, in actuality their power is still great. The status of the psychologist rises in direct proportion to the number of tests used. Psychologists who have eschewed tests have lost status in schools. Psychologists who have clung to their tests have retained the mystique surrounding their evaluations. A test reduces nearly anything to numbers, and numbers give the illusion of exactness. The illusion is what people like. It allows them to hide their opinions in a smoke screen of precision.

When a psychologist says that a student's IQ score is 85, people act as if that means something beyond a simple score. They treat the child as if his school life and his value as a human being are below average, like a vegetable passed over at the supermarket. Chapter 6 deals with the use and misuse of tests, but for right now, remember that the mysticism of the psychologist and ultimately decisions about children's lives are inexorably linked to the phenomenal power of the numbers provided by tests.

BECOMING A SCHOOL PSYCHOLOGIST

I was trained as a school psychologist in the mid-1970s at Indiana University of Pennsylvania (IUP). Having come from New York state, which did not at that time recognize learning disabilities (LD) as a handicap, I had never heard of LD, but soon I was indoctrinated in LD theory, for I was required to take a class titled "Learning Disabilities." I was intrigued by the course name. What exactly were those disabilities that affected a child's brain? It took me many years to find out that it was all guesswork on the part of educators.

I worked hard at trying to understand LD. I listened intently to the discussions in class and read all the assignments; nevertheless I could not shake the feelings of uncertainty about learning disabilities. I was overcome with the vague jargon and ill-defined terms. I could not understand what a learning disability was. The definition itself made little sense to me. The generally accepted definition of LD was

> "Specific Learning Disability" means a disorder in one or more of the basic psychological processes involved in understanding or using language, spoken or written, which may manifest itself in an imperfect ability to listen, think, speak, read, write, spell, or to do mathematical calculations. [1]

One vague term was defined by other vague terms. Why was it called a *specific* learning disability? What is a *disorder*? And what is a *basic psychological process*? What was even more perplexing to me, my classmates all seemed to understand. I did not want to let on that I was too dumb to understand, so I played along and got an A in the class, figuring that when I became a school psychologist I would learn about LD students first hand. There must be LD students out there, surely no one would make up such a thing. I just didn't know they existed before. Armed with my trusty test kits though, I was willing to go looking.

Sometimes experience is the best teacher, and believe me, experience taught me a lot about LD, but it took me a long time. If I was a slow learner, I cannot entirely fault myself. The training system, which presents a certain worldview, was at fault. It emphasized individual deviance as the only explanation for student failure. The deviance may be caused by faulty genes or by background, but the problems belong to the child not to the educational system.

People currently conducting assessments and the professors training others to conduct assessments have all been steeped in the belief system of testing for deviance. A person indoctrinated in a certain way of thinking usually does not change since she has unconsciously adopted the belief system associated with that thinking. Educators are no exception, nor was I an exception. I believed the experts knew what they were talking about.

THE BELIEFS ABOUT TESTING

All psychological testing is based on a psychometric belief system, and psychological practitioners have accepted the facts generated by those tests. Like a perpetual motion machine, beliefs of the professors and textbook writers are handed down to the students. In the face of contradictory evidence, the truth is ignored. Special education has not worked; IQ scores change sometimes drastically; many tests are invalid; labeling is harmful; but those facts are ignored. What is emphasized over and over in undergraduate and graduate schools is that the typical special education problems are within the children and tests will find the faults.

When I graduated from IUP in 1975, I began my career as a school psychologist as most novices begin, as if I knew what I was doing. But I didn't. What I thought I knew was that LD children had minimal brain dysfunction (MBD), that they reversed letters, that they had difficulty sitting still, that they were distractible, and that they had little concept of time and space. Those problems were caused by a fault within the brain, perhaps stemming from birth trauma or a prolonged disease. I knew that all I had to do to diagnose LD students was to give them an IQ test; some visual perception tests, such as the Bender Gestalt or the Frostig; and achievement tests, such as the Woodcock Reading Mastery Test or the Key Math Test. Occasionally, I might give some tests of auditory perception, such as the Goldman-Fristoe-Woodcock Test of Auditory Reception. The results would make clear to me if a child were truly LD. I quickly found that it was not that simple. I followed all of the recommended procedures, but the LD stuff still didn't make sense to me. For weeks, I tested children. None of the scores pointed to a true LD child. I still thought that they were out there. I just hadn't found one yet.

A BOY NAMED LARRY

Eventually, I tested a boy named Larry who was in second grade. He provided an almost perfect fit to the profile of an LD youngster—average intelligence, easy to talk to, difficulty sitting still, serious reading problems, good at mathematics. His teacher was frustrated. She couldn't break through the hardened exterior in which he encased himself.

Larry received a grade level score of 1.2 in word recognition on the Woodcock Reading Mastery Test, far below his placement at 2.6 grade level. He identified only a few of 220 sight words (such as on, of, the), indicating very beginning reading skills. He also scored very low on a test of visual perception and low on most other hand-eye coordination tasks. Those scores were in sharp contrast to his above average IQ score on The Wechsler Intelligence Scale for Children-Revised and his above-average score on a math achievement test. It looked as if I had finally found an LD youngster.

I held a conference with Larry's parents to inform them of the results of the testing. While I discussed LD theory, I mentioned that a family history of reading problems was also a symptom of a learning disability. I asked if there was a history of reading problems in the family. After some probing, Larry's father admitted that he could not read at all. Larry's mother also confessed that she had difficulty reading and never read to the children. That was the decisive confirmation for me. After two months on the job, I had found what the experts were talking about—average intelligence, low reading ability, signs of hyperactivity, perceptual problems, and a family history of reading problems. I had finally found an LD youngster!

Despite Larry's obvious need for help, the parents balked at the LD label. It did not matter anyhow since LD classes were not mandated in those days and the school district did not have an LD program until fourth grade. During fourth and fifth grades, the school district provided full-time LD classes, believing that any LD student would be fixed up and returned to regular education after completing those two years of specialized instruction. That was part of the original supposing about LD—find them, teach them to compensate for their weaknesses, and return them to regular education. Once I found Larry, I began to find others like him.

A GIRL NAMED TINA

A few days later, I received a request from the kindergarten teacher in the same school that Larry attended to evaluate a girl named Tina. Tina was one of the most appealing and hard-to-forget students I have ever encountered. Her straight, black hair and soft, white skin provided the perfect backdrop for her large, dark eyes. Perhaps the similarities between her looks and those of my daughter, who was about the same age, attracted me to her. Regardless, Tina was unforgettable. She was shy but displayed an alluring smile that belied her underlying uneasiness. She responded well to the individual attention she received and was a joy to be with.

The first part of the evaluation went well. Tina scored above average on the Stanford Binet Intelligence Scale. Her scores on most of the other tests were well below what might have been predicted based on the intelligence test. Her ability to copy designs on the Bender Gestalt Visual Motor Test showed classic reversal problems. She scored more like a child half her age than the six year old she was. She struggled desperately to write her name, writing a T, a backward N, an I and an A. The letters, approximately four inches high, were shakily written and sloped severely down and to the right so that none of the letters was on the same line.

Even though she had attended kindergarten for nearly seven months, she identified fewer than five letters of the alphabet. She could not even identify the letters of her own name except for the A. Her teacher also said that Tina had a great deal of difficulty sitting still. Her human figure drawing was less than an inch high on an 8 1/2-by-11-inch paper. This classic sign of insecurity and low self-esteem was probably caused by her difficulties in school I surmised.

Even more significant, I thought, Tina was Larry's sister. The same Larry whom I had called LD and whom the parents did not want labeled. The same Larry whose father could not read. The same Larry who could not get into an LD class anyhow until he was in fourth grade. LD runs in families according to the experts and here was the second offspring of a nonreader. In fact, Tina's problems were far more severe than Larry's, and her scores were proportionally far lower. I had found another LD youngster!

Being a novice, I was befuddled. There was no LD program until fourth grade. Would the parents be any more willing to allow Tina to be labeled LD when she was only in kindergarten? Even if they allowed it, the school had no program for Tina until she was in fourth grade. What should I do?

Well, I knew she could not go to first grade because of the severity of her problems, so I decided not to tell anybody about my

initial diagnosis that Tina was LD. Instead, I told the kindergarten teacher that Tina just hadn't been ready when she came to
school—that she was going to have to repeat kindergarten. Some
children mature more slowly than others I offered, and Tina was
a late bloomer. I wrote my report making that recommendation
and met with the parents. Surely they could wait another year
before anyone told them that Tina was LD; that she and Larry
were suffering from the same disease—probably the same disease
that had caused the father not to be able to read.

Tina repeated kindergarten with the same teacher. During
the next school year, I visited Tina's classroom fully expecting
Tina to have the same problems she had the previous spring. To
my surprise, the teacher said Tina had made remarkable
improvement. She was near the top of her class in all areas. She
knew the alphabet and was in a small group of youngsters who
were receiving reading instruction in kindergarten. Tina's
distractible nature had disappeared.

"OK," I thought. "Wait until first grade. Surely when real
school begins she will have difficulty." I waited until mid-year
before going to visit the first-grade teacher. Tina was doing
exceptionally well in first grade, also. She was in the top reading
group and was getting A's and B's in all subjects. That was
wonderful, but this LD thing had to start bogging her down
shortly. I'll check in second grade. I mean, after all, I was taught
that LD children were wired up wrong that they suffered from
brain damage. LD doesn't sound like something that goes away
like a cold or the flu. Surely no one could overcome something as
serious as brain damage merely by repeating kindergarten. The
tests had showed all the symptoms—distractibility, hyperactivity, hand-eye coordination problems, perceptual errors in a
student of above-average ability.

Second grade came and went. Tina did well there, also. In
fact, Tina continued through elementary school in the top
reading group getting mostly A's and B's during those six years.
No one in the school ever knew that Tina could have been labeled
LD in kindergarten. Tina has been successful in all that she has
tried. She was crowned queen of the local festival and has
graduated from high school near the top of her class. Thank
goodness the school district did not have LD classes until fourth
grade, or I might have called her LD in kindergarten and condemned her to a life as a second-class citizen.

LEARNING MY LESSONS SLOWLY

The lessons I learned from Tina and other students like her began teaching me about LD. I had always been confused by the jargon—minimal brain dysfunction, organicity, distractibility. One question I could not avoid: How could a student, such as Tina, whose brain was wired up wrong get so good in academics so quickly without special instruction? There was no sand tracing, no air writing, no Frostig materials, no special education placement, no IEP, in fact, no LD interventions of any kind, yet her disability went away.

Perhaps there was something wrong in my evaluation but I doubted that. I had always been exacting in my adherence to standardized testing requirements. I always administered tests strictly according to instructions. Tina's success in school caused me to speculate on LD theory itself. Perhaps LD theory was wrong. Perhaps the children just were not ready for what we had been asking them to do. Perhaps the inability to perform some task, such as identifying letters, did not mean a disability. Tina was doing all of the tasks that she could not do a year before. I surmised that having a mother and father who could not read caused Tina to miss out on opportunities to become familiar with letters and numbers. Since she was inexperienced in school related tasks, she appeared, in comparison to others her age, to be disabled. All Tina needed was the opportunity in a safe environment to experience letters and numbers successfully. Too often though, students like Tina become the victims of poor teaching, poor curriculum, or poor materials.

During the mid-1970s when LD was not mandated, I evaluated many children like Larry and Tina in kindergarten through third grade who were unable to read well—many of whom could have been called LD. Since there were no LD services available, I had children repeat a grade or had the teacher try different teaching strategies or different materials. Most of the children improved greatly from one year to the next. The school districts in which I worked had very few LD youngsters in them. I was even accused by one LD teacher of trying to help the administration save money by doing away with LD programs.

QUESTIONING LD THEORY

Undaunted, I seriously began to question LD theory. Tina was not the only child I encountered who overcame her symptoms of LD without any direct instruction, merely the first. I was not one to place a label, any label, on a child until I was absolutely sure that there were no alternatives. The more students I tested, the more confused I became. I found that most of the children I had tested, upon retesting could do the things that I had said they could not do on previous evaluations. If they were truly disabled, why were they able to do things they were unable to do previously? A blind child can't see a year later. A deaf child can't hear a year later. Why could brain-damaged children do things they could not do a year earlier?

The answer eluded me for a while because I was so steeped in the belief system of special education I did not really understand how we in special education were viewing children. I began reading every book I could find on learning disabilities and early childhood education. Three books, in particular, greatly impressed me. The titles alone tell you what they are about—*School Can Wait*,[2] *Better Late Than Early*,[3] and *Don't Push Your Preschooler*.[4] I was led to regard early experiences as an important link in discovering what causes scholastic underachievement. The lockstep admissions system based on chronological age seemed to be forcing children into school before some of them were ready. Once there, they were herded into groups and labeled as at-risk if they did not perform like other youngsters.

Not only did I read, I began talking to the people with whom I worked. The reading specialist in one of the districts in which I worked, charted the birthdays of the children enrolled in special education and Title I compensatory programs. She found that the younger children in each grade were the ones most often enrolled in those remedial programs. In particular, a boy born in the last quarter of the year was almost assured of being placed in a remedial reading or math program. The majority of boys in the school system whose birthdays were in the last quarter of the year were enrolled in remedial or compensatory programs. Many children, it seemed, were failing because they were too inexperienced for the demands of schooling. There was a more complete answer than that, however.

THE ANSWER

The complete answer became obvious to me gradually as I worked with more and more young children. We, in education, were viewing children as being at fault. We saw the handicaps and failures as being in the children. The schools, the teachers, the curricula, the instruction were never considered as being at fault. As a school psychologist, I was employed to determine what was wrong with the children. No one was employed to determine what was wrong with the curricula, materials, or techniques used to teach the children. It was assumed that those things were above suspicion, but the more I read, the more I realized that the curricula, materials, and techniques including the rush to school, may have been to blame. I began to change my thinking and started looking elsewhere for clues about LD.

I ultimately concluded that LD children were children who had encountered difficulties in schooling much like one might encounter difficulty hitting a golf ball or riding a horse. Given time to grow and with proper instruction under the right circumstances, golf ball hitting or horseback riding would improve and so would reading, ciphering, and spelling.

If what I surmised were correct, the notion of LD being some sort of brain dysfunction was incorrect. I began looking at where the LD ideas came from to help point the way out of my confusion.

NOTES

1. U. S. Office of Education. (1977). Education of handicapped children: Implementation of part B of the education of handicapped act. *Federal Register*, 42(163), August 23, p. 42,475.

2. Moore, R. S., Moore, D. N. et al. (1979). *School can wait*. Provo, UT: Brigham Young Press.

3. Moore, R. S. (1977). *Better late than early: A new approach to your child's education.* New York: Reader's Digest Press.

4. Ames, L. B., & Chase, J. A. (1980). *Don't push your preschooler.* New York: Harper & Row.

4

What Is LD and Where Did It Come From?

There is nothing so powerful as an idea whose time has come.
Victor Hugo

In the 1960s, an idea whose time had definitely come was the notion of learning disabilities. It was an idea that had been kicked around since the late 1800s using various terms—the earliest of which was *word blindness*. Over the years, many terms had been used to describe essentially the same phenomenon, including *perceptual handicap, neurological impairment, dyslexia, minimal brain damage, multiple brain dysfunction*—eventually evolving to the less noxious and more evasive term *learning disabilities*. Until the middle 1960s the condition was virtually unheard of. Since then, the term has been so eagerly applied to children that nearly everybody knows someone who is LD, and everybody has some idea of what they think LD means. Usually the ideas are vague and misguided.

THE BIRTH OF A DISEASE

The term *learning disabilities* first appeared in print in 1962. It came into general use when Samuel Kirk, who was serving as director of the Division of Exceptional Children and Youth in the U.S. Office of Education, interpreted another special education term *other health impaired* to include learning disabilities. The ultimate acceptance of the term came from political pressure applied by middle-class parents of underachieving youngsters. They pressured the federal legislature to recognize underachievement in certain students as a handicap caused by neurological dysfunction. The parents organized, as most political movements do, and enlisted the support of educational professionals. By 1969, the parents had mustered the professional support needed to legitimize LD. Congress, bowing to the will of the people, recognized LD as a handicap by passing the Children with Learning Disabilities Act of 1969, which led to the funding of five LD research institutions. The institutions were to provide training and research regarding LD. In practical terms, once the law was passed, LD moved from theory into reality.

Following the passage of that law, the growth of LD was rapid. The growth could be traced to the theory itself. There was strong appeal in the notion that difficulty in school was organic, a tiny malfunction in the brain, not the least of which was the seeming blamelessness of LD theory. LD theory lets everyone off the hook—parents, teachers, and students—while giving an apparent explanation for failure to learn. It was serendipitous that the LD movement came along on the coattails of the civil rights movement of the 1960s and was fed by it.

CIVIL RIGHTS MOVEMENT

Civil rights was the political hot potato of the 1960s. Discrimination against minorities was real. The middle class, demanding rights for their children who were not reading, and based on analogy, saw another minority being discriminated against—their children. The parents banded together, much like civil rights activists, and demanded that LD theory be recognized as a real condition. Unfortunately, LD theory was no more than supposition. The supposing was the kind of thinking that may help move science toward truth but is not truth. The problem was that learning disabilities theory was still in its infancy and was based more on analogy than on fact. Regardless, special interest groups gained political clout in much the same way that the civil rights activists did and embraced the notion of LD. There was no doubt that handicapped people, as well as minorities, needed protection. LD, by getting itself included as a handicap, benefited from a major political force, and, on the basis of legislation brought about by political activism, *LD theory became law without evidence.* LD's place in educational history was legitimized and sanctioned as real.

The fact that no convincing evidence for the existence of LD has ever been put forth has not dissuaded the believers. Instead, the thinking has been changed. LD is no longer viewed by the experts as a brain dysfunction. It is now viewed as a heterogenous concept. Any disturbing behavior—disturbing to some adults, that is—would or could allow a student to be labeled as LD.

WHAT DO THE EXPERTS SAY
LEARNING DISABILITIES ARE?

The most frequently used definition of learning disabilities was developed in 1968 by the National Advisory Committee on Handicapped Children and was adopted by the federal government in The Education of All Handicapped Children Act (PL 94-142) with virtually no changes. Part of the definition was quoted in chapter 3. The entire PL 94-142 definition is as follows:

> "Specific Learning Disability" means a disorder in one or more of the basic psychological processes involved in understanding or using language, spoken or written, which may manifest itself in an imperfect ability to listen, think, speak, read, write, spell, or to do mathematical calculations. The term includes such conditions as perceptual handicaps, brain injury, minimal brain dysfunction, dyslexia, and developmental aphasia. The term does not include children who have learning problems which are primarily the result of visual, hearing, or motor handicaps, of mental retardation, or of environmental, cultural or economic disadvantage. [1]

As I mentioned in chapter 3, the definition is confusing and full of holes. Nowhere does the law explain what constitutes a disorder or what psychological processes are, much less what a *basic* psychological process is; and, I would guess that all of us have some version of that "imperfect ability to listen, think, speak, read, write, spell, or to do mathematical calculations." The law was guilty of defining a vague term with several other vague terms, but no one complained. Otherwise, there would be no LD definition because agreement could not be reached on a concrete definition. In fact, more than twenty-five years later a satisfactory definition still has not been put forth. Educational journals abound with articles about the difficulties in trying to define LD. Nearly every textbook on LD begins with some version of the following:

> Learning disabilities, though very real, remain an intriguing puzzle. This is true, even though they officially

received their name during the mid-1960s.... The term *learning disabilities* has different meanings to individuals in different professions. It may also have different meanings to individuals within the same profession. One expert in the field of special education noted that "the field [learning disabilities] is in obvious turmoil, if not disarray. We move to an uncertain future, but when was that not true? We are at least not afflicted with the illusion of constancy and stability."[2]

I wonder how many parents of LD children truly understand that the term applied to their children by experts is viewed as an "intriguing puzzle"; that experts in the same professions don't agree as to what LD is; that people in different fields see the problem differently; that the field is in "obvious turmoil if not disarray"; that there is no "illusion of stability" in the field. Would parents want such a negative label applied to their children only to provide them with an "uncertain future?"

Even a cursory look at some definitions of learning disabilities demonstrates the enormity of the problem of attempting to understand the true nature of learning disabilities. Janet Lerner's text on LD, which I used for the LD course I took in 1974, had no fewer than seven definitions within five broad categories.[3] One is left with the immediate question, "How can a single disease have so many definitions?" Well, the answer has to do with the definitions themselves. The definitions mentioned by Lerner use terms, such as *developmental imbalances, psychological processes, cerebral dysfunction,* and *essential learning processes.* Defining an ambiguous term with other vague terms merely begs the question. One would have to be a certain type of masochist to even attempt to differentiate essential learning processes from nonessential learning processes, just as it makes no sense to speak of cerebral dysfunction. At least brain dysfunction would name an organ that might be capable of dysfunctioning.   And, if we do not know what a learning disability is, we certainly do not know what developmental imbalances are. They sound like something that might happen to washing machines in the spin cycle.

The federal definition, although it is vague, certainly views the problem as being an attribute of the child. The movement views LD as a "disease by default, the medical ailment which can be ascribed to those children who have no other problems but who don't learn to talk or read as their elders think they should."[4]   Children have difficulty learning, the thinking goes, because of something inside of them, and we can only study it and try to explain it.   What that it is, is the problem.   Virtually no one looks outside the child to see LD as an educational problem.

The federal definition adopted in 1977 is still in use—a definition so vague that many different conclusions could be reached regarding what is meant.   Cutting through all the gibberish, it seems the definition states that some students achieve below what they could be expected to achieve, and, if that underachievement cannot be accounted for because they are blind, deaf, retarded, or deprived, in theory then, it might be concluded that the underachievement is caused by something within the child—a disability. The problem with such a vague definition is that being unable to properly define a disease makes it easy to misidentify, for only through a clearly defined set of criteria can identifications be made.   LD has no clearly defined criteria, and nearly anyone can sneak in with such nonsense.

One of the problems with the definition is that the emphasis is on what LD is not. The last sentence of the definition says, "The term does not include children who have learning problems which are primarily the result of visual, hearing, or motor handicaps, of mental retardation, or of environmental, cultural, or economic disadvantage." The emphasis is on the ruling out of causes. We cannot define LD by telling what it is not anymore than we can define a chair by saying it is not a table, a desk, a dresser, a rug, or even a tractor.   Emphasizing what something is not never leads to what it is.

RULING OUT CAUSES

Despite the foolishness of defining what something is not, this ruling out causes is one of the basic premises of LD. As the thinking goes, once other possible causes of underachievement have been ruled out, it might be concluded that something within the child, a neurological disorder, has caused the learning problem. No consideration is given to poor teaching, lousy curriculum, boring subjects, or lack of motivation. The neurological disorder that caused the LD is like a computer glitch, an electronic malfunction. It may be so minimal that we cannot find it, but it is still there, still within the child not within the educational system. Since the glitch is unable to be easily detected, we can exclude virtually no one from LD consideration.

One of the most interesting aspects of ruling out causes is ruling out the concept of environmental disadvantage. We could spend an eternity trying to rule it out as a cause of LD. Environmental disadvantage, like beauty, is in the eyes of the beholder. Too much TV, too little of the right TV (like "Mr. Rogers"); parents who work, parents who don't work; too many brothers and sisters, no one to play with; inner city living, rural living—the list is nearly endless and contradictory. Even more to the point, if LD runs in families and the parents can't read, then hasn't the child suffered an environmental disadvantage by being raised in a home in which there is no reading?

To make matters worse, in some cases, the very causes that may exclude a student from LD consideration also may not exclude him. I know that doesn't make sense but it is a practical reality. Experts agree that exclusionary causes may be present but must be a consequence of, not a cause of, the disability. For example, emotional disturbance must be ruled out as a cause of underachievement before the LD label can be applied to a student, but emotional disturbance may also be the result of underachievement. Therefore, any underachieving student who is emotionally disturbed is not excluded from LD consideration since it cannot be concluded whether the disturbance resulted from the underachievement or whether the underachievement resulted from the disturbance. Since no one can say which came first—the emotional disturbance or the learning disability—nearly anyone who is labeled emotionally disturbed may be labeled LD.

Furthermore, the presence of retardation is not always an exclusionary condition even though LD, by definition, is for average and above average students only. It is often argued that a low IQ score may be caused by some neurological inability to respond to the evaluation questions on the IQ tests. Thus, the floodgates are opened because the LD definition is insufficient to exclude anyone. That is the main difficulty with the LD definition. It is so loose and has been applied to such a large pool of students who are underachievers in the determinations of who is LD, that it seldom rules out anyone. Instead, like the Statue of Liberty, LD programs are clamoring for education's "poor, tired, huddled masses." Only under the most unusual of cases is any attempt made to rule out other causes.

BLAMING THE CHILDREN

The federal LD definition, although it is vague, certainly views the problem as being an attribute of the child. The movement views LD as a disease by default: When we can't figure out what to do, label and segregate children who have no other problems except they don't talk, read, or cipher as well as adults think they should. Since children have difficulty learning, the thinking goes, because of something inside of them, we can only study that something and try to explain it. What that it is, is the problem. Virtually no one looks outside the child and sees LD as being an educational problem.

Blaming the children was the primary notion of the LD theorizing that produced the PL 94-142 thinking. The requirements varied but tried to produce the view of the child as the cause of the learning problems. For example, until 1978, anyone labeled as LD in Pennsylvania was required to be evaluated by a physician for neurological problems. Virtually none of the children referred to doctors were ever found to have neurological problems. That alone should have stopped them from being admitted to LD programs. Instead family doctors and pediatricians obliged the parents and the schools by writing perfunctory letters or notes saying that they had screened the student for neurological problems. The letters never mentioned the results of the screenings because they usually found nothing. The schools accepted the letters as meeting the requirements, and the neurological screening hurdle was overcome. When the State Standards for Special Education were rewritten in 1978, that requirement was removed because it did nothing to discourage LD enrollment.

Why did the doctors not find anything in the neurological screenings that they performed during the 1970s? The obvious answer is that there was nothing to find since most research has not been able to confirm neurological and perceptual theories. That is not the answer offered by the believers. They merely suggested that the neurological problems were truly minimal, so minimal that they could not be detected. The students' brains were dysfunctional rather than damaged. When you can't find what you set out to find, then chance your requirements, but for heaven sake don't change your theory.

LOOKING AT PL 94-142

PL 94-142, passed in 1975, brought with it the recognition of LD as a legitimate handicap using the federal LD definition previously cited. LD took its place along side blindness, deafness, mental retardation, and physical handicaps as a legal disability. Turning a theory into a law and requiring a bureaucracy as big as education to administer it pretty much assured LD's growth and acceptance. Schools were only too willing to remove their least able from regular classrooms and to provide them with a special education. Classroom teachers were relieved of the burden of dealing with underachievers, and administrators could make parents and teachers happy while using rooms left vacant by the overall enrollment decline of the post baby boom years.

The problem with PL 94-142, as with most federal education legislation, was that it was a financial tease. The federal government gives a few dollars and requires massive changes in return. Education is a state, rather than a federal responsibility, so ultimately the states were to decide if they would accept federal dollars from PL 94-142. Once they did, they were required to assume the primary policy-making and financial responsibilities regarding the education of handicapped students. The problem with accepting federal funding is that the federal government has never funded more than 10 percent of the provisions of PL 94-142, yet, when states accepted federal funds, they were obligated to comply with all provisions of the law, including the recognition of LD as a handicap.

THE PREVALENCE OF LD

The impact of PL 94-142 on LD was rapid. In the seven years following its passage, LD grew 127 percent. That growth is profound, but it was even more pronounced when compared to the 12 percent decrease in the total school population in those same years and the 13 percent decrease in students labeled as handicapped when LD is excluded as a category. Although the growth rate has subsided, the number of LD students in the U.S., has increased every year since 1975.

Education, being a state responsibility, provides different classification systems and different criteria for identification of LD students from state to state. This variation in state classification systems based on fiscal and philosophic differences has produced considerable differences across states in the numbers of LD students served in special education. In 1985, for example, Indiana had identified only 3 percent of its population as being LD while Rhode Island had labeled 8.7 percent of its population as LD, nearly triple. States with large populations varied as much as did states with small populations. What has produced the differences by state?

Two of the major conclusions reached by one study were (a) that the more it costs state and local districts for LD services, the fewer handicapped children they identify; and (b) if there were no financial incentives to identify LD students, then fewer students were labeled as LD than in states with higher financial incentives.[5] In effect, money was buying the label for some children. If they moved to another state, those same children might not be LD. Whether you like it or not, local and state bureaucrats seemed to be applying the label to certain kids so that their states or school districts could get more money.

IS LD REALLY A NEW GROUP OF STUDENTS?

Another concern offered by some LD thinkers was that the tremendous increase in LD students may have been the result of a large group of children who were not being served prior to the 1970s, but that does not seem to be the case. By 1989, 48 percent of the total of 4.1 million handicapped youngsters were called LD. Prior to the mid 1960s, there were no LD youngsters.

With the growth in the number of LD youngsters came a decrease in the youngsters served by Chapter I remedial math and reading compensatory programs. From 1966 to 1983 the number of disadvantaged children served by Chapter I had decreased by 1.5 million while LD children had grown to 1.8 million. (Mentally retarded decreased by 220,000 during that same period making up most of the difference.) Students who, in the past, may have been called academically disadvantaged were now being called disabled. A new label had been discovered for reading failure. The Chapter I disadvantaged programs and the programs for mildly handicapped were serving students who were remarkably similar in many ways and could not be distinguished in any consistent way from each other. In the schools where I worked as school psychologist, Chapter I reading and math were prerequisites on the road to LD. Students who were having trouble reading were sent to the Chapter I teacher. If they did not improve, they were referred for a special education evaluation to determine eligibility for LD.

PERMANENT VERSUS TEMPORARY

The greatest tragedy with the change from disadvantaged to disabled was the change in attitude. Disadvantaged implies temporary; disabled implies permanence. The view of under-achievement as being a permanent rather than temporary state has much to do with the classification models used to describe underachievement. The next chapter deals with those classification models.

NOTES

1. U. S. Office of Education. (1977). Education of handicapped children: Implementation of part B of the education of handicapped act. *Federal Register*, 42(163), August 23, p. 42,475.

2. Gearheart, B. R., & Gearheart, C. J. (1989). *Learning disabilities: Educational strategies*. Columbus: Merrill, p. 3.

3. Lerner, J. W. (1971). *Children with learning disabilities: Theories, diagnosis, and teaching strategies*. New York: Houghton Mifflin.

4. Schrag, P., & Divoky, D. (1975). *The myth of the hyperactive child*. New York: Dell, p. 45.

5. Noel, M. M., & Fuller, B. C. (1985). The social policy construction of special education: The impact of state characteristics on identification and integration of handicapped children. *Remedial and Special Education*, 6(3), 27-35.

5

LD Classification Models

What you see is what you get.
Popular expression

How we look at things determines to a great extent what we see. The classification of students as LD is no exception. Most disciplines have a set of beliefs that helps shape what practitioners look at. Optometrists tend to see LD as a visual perception problem; neurologists tend to see LD as brain related; audiologists tend to see LD as an auditory perception problem. Sociologists look at the social aspects of the problem. Psychologists look at the psychological aspects of the disorder. Their beliefs are often developed into models that serve as a framework from which to view LD.

EDUCATIONAL MODELS

Many competing models have been used in education to describe student underachievement. Two models, in particular, have led to much confusion regarding learning disabilities: the medical model and the social systems model. The medical model has been used to describe underachievement. The medical model uses many medical terms, allowing education to take on the form of medicine. We talk of diagnostic and prescriptive teaching, referrals, follow-up, therapists, counselors, clinical supervision, and the like, unconsciously believing that what we are talking about is, in reality, medical in nature. The category of LD is a paramount example of the medicalized thinking in education. LD theory came as a offshoot of medical theory about how the brain works and was allowed to flourish regardless of the fact that virtually everything that was believed about LD and its brain-caused origins has remained unproven. Because of the lack of proof regarding brain theories and LD, much of the current thinking about LD has shifted into a social systems model that has blurred the distinctions between the two competing models. In many respects, the two models are not compatible.

THE MEDICAL MODEL

The medical model looks at what are supposed to be biological symptoms in a dichotomous fashion to determine disease. If symptoms are present, the subject is considered to be abnormal or diseased. A biopsy, for example, reveals the presence of malignant cells. If malignant cells are found, the person has cancer—no malignancy, no cancer. According to the medical model, pathological symptoms are caused by biological conditions. Sociocultural influences are not relevant to diagnosis or treatment. The treatment is not culture-bound. Chemotherapy should be equally effective with Australians as with Americans, Mexicans, or Tibetans.

Pathology is an attribute of the person and may exist unrecognized. The ethical code of medical practitioners would say that errors should be made on the side of overdiagnosis. It is better to have false positives than false negatives. That is, it is better to treat someone who does not have cancer than not to treat someone who has cancer.

LD from the medical point of view is seen as pathology, as being within the child. LD is seen in a dichotomous fashion, either someone has it, or she does not. People tend to believe that the symptoms of LD exist independent of culture. If children are "wired up wrong," the thinking goes, they are equally detectible in the American classroom or in the Australian bush. The behavior of the child is like a runny nose. A symptom allows the inference of underlying causes. Terms, such as *diagnosis, intervention,* and *symptom* express and, ultimately, form people's viewpoints. Overdiagnosing LD is seen as a good thing. It is better to be safe than sorry.

THE SOCIAL SYSTEMS MODEL

The second model that can be applied to learning problems is the social systems model. This model views abnormality as deviance from the norm. Abnormal behavior violates social systems. In this model, local values determine abnormality. In different communities and different cultures, varying behaviors are viewed as abnormal. Biology is not a consideration. Deviance becomes a social judgment and cannot exist unrecognized. Because of the punitive nature of the resulting labels applied by judgments, it is better to have more false negatives than false positives. It is better to say students are not deviant when they are, than to say they are deviant when they are not.

When original LD theory could not be confirmed in practice, a subtle shift occurred in the thinking so that LD became viewed as deviance from the norm, and, in effect, part of a social system. However, most of the other assumptions of the social systems model were ignored, especially the punitive nature of labels, leading to a merging of the two models. This integration of the two models led to the view of deviance not just as abnormality, but as disease.

DEVIANCE AS DISEASE

LD is only one of many terms being applied to people in increasing fashion giving the false impression that science has somehow ordained those categories. Alcoholism, drug addiction, compulsive gambling, and eating disorders are some others. Language is the device used to segment and ultimately control portions of the population that do not conform to preconceived definitions of rightness, correctness, or health—conformity being the right and correct manner in which to act or think. Deviation, therefore, becomes disease by definition. The underlying assumptions are based on supposedly scientific findings that are usually little more than the conjecture of psychologists, psychiatrists, and educators trying to make names for themselves at the expense of others. The labeling of people as deviant and thus defective is the McCarthyism of the 1980s and 1990s. If your children do not act or think as experts believe they should, they are labeled as deviant under the guise of science and honesty.

LD is based on the notion that if one student is different from his peers by very much, he will be labeled as defective. The social systems model warns of the punitive nature of the labels and suggests underidentification is preferable. The great tragedy is that the medical model has been followed in overlabeling LD children, providing them with labels that may follow them for the rest of their lives. Practitioners believe they are providing help for students if they label, so borderline and ineligible students are labeled as well.

The idea of deviance as disease has forced people to view the least able as defective, but it has also forced us to view the most able as being equally defective. Some psychologists suggest that too much of a good thing, such as honesty, can be bad. The Minnesota Multiphasic Personality Inventory (MMPI), a personality test used to measure a series of traits based on self-reporting provides a cogent example. Items on the MMPI are of the following type:

> I am often upset or agitated.
> I make friends easily.
> I blame others when things go wrong.

Someone taking the test must tell to what degree each of the statements is true as she sees herself. One of the problems with self-reporting measures is that people tend to distort the truth to appear as they think they should. To counteract the effects of distorting, the MMPI has a lie scale. The assumption is that no one is perfect, that we all distort to some degree. The question is: How much will each person distort? That question is answered by assuming that if a person's responses are not similar to most people's responses, then the person might be lying and the rest of the test should be regarded as suspect. High moral character is indicted as deviance just as is weak moral character. The lying probes are like the following:

> I have stolen candy from a store.
> If I knew I would not get caught, I would sneak into a movie theater.

The test's authors assume that everyone has stolen candy or would sneak into a movie. If a person truly has never stolen candy, or if she would not sneak into a movie under any circumstances, and she answers the questions honestly, she is not like most people. Being too honest is interpreted as being dishonest. Therefore, she is thought to be a liar. Such is the way psychology has ineptly led us. Deviation from the norm in either direction, even deviation in a positive direction, may mark her as sick.

DISTRUSTING OUR INSTINCTS

Those of you not well acquainted with what has been written about LD may think I am off base with my assertions—but listen to what others have said about viewing deviance as disease:

> It is a gradual, subtle and seductive process, but the political and social consequences are enormous. When the impositions come in the name of diagnosis and treatment ("for the benefit of the child"), not in the name of punishment and control, otherwise arbitrary institutional procedures begin to look reasonable and the power to manipulate is immeasurably enhanced. This is science talking, it is the natural order of things; what are we (sic) doing to you has nothing to do with the arbitrary decisions of school administrators or cops or the social bias of the community. As a consequence it becomes increasingly hard to resist, increasingly tempting to go along with, and increasingly difficult for the individual—parent or child—even to know exactly what is happening or why. What is certain is that the new ideology and the associated techniques—screens, drugs, behavior modification, special programs—all serve the purpose of legitimizing and enlarging the power of institutions over individuals. *In every instance it is argued that for this individual case, the "treatment" is preferable to the alternatives.... An entire generation is slowly being conditioned to distrust its own instincts, to regard its deviation from narrowing standards or approved norms as sickness and to rely on the institutions of the state and on technology to define and engineer its "health"* (italics added).[1]

It is easy to be taken in by the subtle and seductive process of regarding "deviation from narrowing standards or approved norms as sickness." Well-meaning teachers, counselors, and psychologists test children and draw conclusions for the benefit of the child. The disease your child may have has nothing to do with anything but the luck of the draw; your child came into the world behind the eight ball. There is no one to argue with since the custodians of the new ideology are on your side. They agree that you and your child are victims. Institutional programming is the only answer. You should let Big Brother take care of you.

In reality, LD is a metaphor, an arbitrary label applied to children and does not exist any more than any other metaphor exists, but the use of the metaphor keeps us from recognizing it as a metaphor and understanding it. LD in practical terms means *underachievement in reading* or sometimes in math or spelling. Even the term *underachievement* is a metaphorical product of language. Labeling actions as nouns leads to the assumption that the noun has become reality. There is no such thing as underachievement; it is a label, a result of language, used as a convenience. In much of education, confusing the real with the imitation obscures meaning until there is none. The problems are not trivial either. Once so defined, a pervasive self-fulfilling prophesy takes hold. The child no longer has to learn, the teacher no longer has to teach, and the parent has an explanation for the relatives.

THE NATURE OF LD

The distortion of what is real by language has produced today's confusion. Mass media reports what makes good copy. Students who cannot read yet have graduated from high school; students who cannot sit still; and students who are seen as being different in some way make good human interest stories. Misdiagnosed or undiagnosed problems make for tear-jerking headlines. Famous people who cannot read make interesting stories. The average person believes what he reads is true including everything the popular media put forth about LD. By way of example, the average person, when asked about the nature of learning disabilities, would reply with an answer mentioning letter and word reversals or brain dysfunction. Perhaps, some friend has it; perhaps mention of a famous person, such as Einstein or Edison who supposedly had undiagnosed cases of it, and some vague talk about compensating for deficits. It would matter little if the person asked were an educator since they have no more understanding of LD research than most other people. None of these descriptions of LD have been proven.[2]
It would matter little if the person being asked were a school psychologist, the workers who most often evaluate and label the students as LD, since they seem to be more responsive to what is expected of them than what is correct. School psychologists deliver their pronouncements in a fashion giving them the status accorded physicians in the healing arts, when in reality

their reports are little more than musings and speculation. However, because of the nature of the psychologists' role and the perceived value of their opinions, few dare question or even consider questioning psychologists' speculations. Instead, their opinions are accepted as virtual fact, and decisions about children's lives are based on their opinions and speculation.

LD AS UNDERACHIEVEMENT

While I believe that LD does not exist in any real sense, I do not mean that the symptoms do not exist. These symptoms can be found in nearly any book regarding LD. The emphasis on symptoms focuses almost exclusively on what is inherently bad about the child. Little is ever said about the educational system in which the student is being educated. Because of that bias, it is almost universally accepted that the problem lies within the child.

Perhaps the best example I can give about the prejudice against children is from *Kids Who Underachieve* by Lawrence Greene.[3] Greene has written at least two other books on education and many would call him an expert. The book in question speaks not just about LD but of the broader category of underachievers. Greene defines the four common sources of underachievement as *learning problems, family problems, emotional problems*, and *cultural influences*. Greene never considers poor teachers and poor curricula leading to underachievement. Even the most cursory of investigations would lead one to conclude that teachers and curricula are major sources of underachievement. All one would have to do is survey average Americans and ask if they ever were underachievers. Most would admit to sometimes not applying themselves in school, and, I believe, most would tell about how certain teachers or subjects turned them off. Most students simply do not work to their potential in some subjects or with some teachers.

Furthermore, if Greene had taken even a casual look at the literature on reading underachievement, he would have encountered Rudolf Flesch's 1955 book *Why Johnny Can't Read—And What You Can Do About It*, one of the most famous books on the ills of faulty instruction.[4] Flesch fingered look-say reading instruction as the primary cause of reading underachievement. Flesch wrote a second book about the same subject in 1981, *Why Johnny Still Can't Read*.[5] Even though Greene's book was published nearly thirty-one years after *Why Johnny Can't Read*, and five years after *Why Johnny Still Can't Read*, Greene never mentioned instructional methods as a possible cause of underachievement. Even if he did not believe that they were causes, ignoring so completely what has been put forth for years in the reading literature goes to show the depth of his the belief that children and their backgrounds are at fault.

Little wonder that we have difficulty understanding underachievement when an expert makes no mention of schools, teachers, and subject matter as possible causes of underachievement. The common causes, according to Greene, are the result of the child's home and heredity, not his teacher or his school. Underachievement is the fault of the child or his family.

Despite what you might believe, research does not bear out Greene's beliefs about underachievement. No one has been able to demonstrate an exclusive link between underachievement and background. Instead, political interest groups have banded together and through legislation have forced beliefs on society that have no basis in fact.

It is also interesting to note that motivation is not mentioned in Greene's book. Surely, motivation is an important component of any achievement, and lack of achievement in many cases can be traced to underachievement. I am not saying that Greene's book is not helpful, for it does discuss some of the other factors involved in underachievement, such as learning not to achieve, self-image, self-esteem, resistance, but it completely ignores much of what can also contribute to underachievement— institutional practices, instructional practices, and poor curriculum.

The twin concepts of deviance equals disease and background causes underachievement require that every child suspected of having a disability be tested. The testing industry is a multimillion dollar enterprise in which much hype and hoopla is afforded new tests. How effective are the tests? The next chapter answers that question.

NOTES

1. Schrag, P., & Divoky, D. (1975). *The myth of the hyperactive child*. New York: Dell, p. 16.
2. Coles, G. (1987). *The learning mystique*. New York: Pantheon.

3. Greene, L. J. (1986). *Kids who underachieve*. New York: Simon & Schuster, p. 46.

4. Flesch, R. (1955). *Why Johnny can't read--and what you can do about it*. New York: Harper.

5. Flesch, R. (1981). *Why Johnny still can't read*. New York: Harper & Row.

6

Testing

God himself, sir, does not propose
to judge man until the end of his days.
Johnson

Paramount in the misguided thinking about LD is the unbridled belief that educational and psychometric tests are capable of measuring what they purport to measure and that they are unfailing in their ability to do so. Of course, special education professionals always acknowledge the limitations of tests in an abstract sense in their journals and textbooks. In concrete applications with individual children, however, seldom are there any serious cautions about the limits of the tests and the conclusions that can be reached using them. Tests are treated as sacrosanct and seen as somehow above suspicion. The high regard that tests are held in is quite evident in the way the scores are treated. Many reports are never read but the scores are quoted at length in the meetings held to discuss children's futures. A brief anecdote illustrates how important test scores are to educationists.

REMOVING AN ERRONEOUS SCORE
FROM A STUDENT'S RECORD

I had a call from a father who wanted an IQ score removed from his son's permanent records. Since I was the administrator in charge, the father was correct in calling me, but it was a call that never should have been made. The score the father wanted removed was from an individually administered IQ test given by one of the psychologists I was supervising at the time. The test was several years old and had been administered prior to the student's enrollment in kindergarten. The child scored so low (an IQ score in the 50s), that he was enrolled in a class for trainable mentally retarded (TMR) children. His parents were told that he could not handle regular kindergarten. In fact, according to the father, they were told that the boy was so low functioning that he would probably never learn to read and write. He would be able to be trained for some low-skill jobs but that was about it.

The father went on to report that over the past six years his son had progressed from TMR to EMR (educable mentally retarded) to regular classes. He had taken several IQ tests, each score increasing over the previous score. His current IQ score was in the low-average range, and he was doing well in school. The same psychologist had administered all evaluations, the low scores and the high scores. The psychologist could see that the original evaluation must have been in error—the boy was in regular class in the sixth grade, getting passing grades. The father was afraid that the test score calling his son retarded might be used against him at a future time, yet the psychologist refused to destroy the first test, the only one that had an IQ score in the retarded range. The father appealed to me for help. I ordered the test results destroyed; but as I said, the call never should have been made. The psychologist, if he was not so enamored with what he saw as the objectivity of test scores, would have destroyed the results himself. The boy was definitely not retarded. The score was wrong, plain and simple.

OBJECTIVE(?) TESTS

Psychoeducational tests are no more objective than the people who make them or the people who use them. Most tests are produced by large corporations whose sole interest is the bottom line—sales. The tests are created to meet perceived needs and are manufactured to produce certain results. Tests have become all-powerful tools used to label and ultimately harm children, all the while pretending objectivity and impartiality. The real purpose of tests is to draw lines. If a child scores above a certain line, the child is normal, average, or not at-risk. If the child scores below that line, she is diseased, handicapped, retarded, disabled, disturbed, at-risk, or any of the other terrible names we call children. The tests are for dividing so we can justify what we do to children.

Educational tests are administered by school psychologists, LD specialists, guidance counselors, and teachers. Those people make decisions about individual students. The decisions are based almost solely on test results despite requirements to use other criteria. The ability of IQ tests, perceptual tests, academic achievement tests, and the like to separate children accurately is unquestionably false. Most of the tests used to determine LD eligibility are unable to provide the information needed to accurately declare someone eligible for LD services, yet the system persists.

SCREENING AND TESTING

Often a child's first encounter with testing is at a very early age. Nowadays, a child who enrolls in kindergarten and has not been tested, evaluated, screened, or subjected to some other form of personal invasion in the name of help is rare. The purpose of those screenings, testings, and evaluations is to single out the deviant—anyone who does something different. It does not matter what. If your son or daughter takes up a pencil with the right hand and later transfers it to the left, it is noted. If he looks at mommy when asked to come with the tester, it is noted. If she is scared or nervous to be with a stranger, it is noted. If he sucks his thumb, picks his nose, twists his hair, or blinks his eyes too often for the examiner's preference, it is noted. Most of the notations are about behaviors. "He was unable to build a three block bridge." "He did not color inside the lines." "She chewed her nails and would not talk unless asked a direct question." "He seldom looked at the examiner." Almost anything that is different from what other children have done is considered a symptom. If the child shows enough symptoms, a formal declaration of disease is made. If a child has some symptoms, but not enough for a formal declaration, she may be evaluated with different tests until enough symptoms are found, or she may be called at-risk with teachers being told to "keep an eye on her."

Once suspicion is thrown a child's way, it rarely is avoided. Some children are given fifteen to thirty tests. At a nearby university, all undergraduate students training to be special education teachers must take a course in individual assessment and must test children whose parents have taken them to the university for such evaluations. Usually, those parents are dissatisfied with what the schools have done and are looking for help. Unfortunately, the help may be based on tests administered by nineteen-and twenty-year-old college students.

Those undergraduate students may never have administered a test in their lives but are entrusted with testing children and generating reports that could significantly affect the lives of those children. The professor usually gives the IQ test (that, of course, is the big one) and allows the students to give all other tests. Sometimes parents are allowed to watch behind a one-way glass. (That is another ploy to convince parents of their child's weaknesses. After all, it is hard to argue that a child can build a three-block bridge when the parents saw that he did not do it. The question about the importance of building a three-block bridge is never raised.)

When a child is having difficulty in school, a parent conference is scheduled. All of the talk and rigmarole usually leads to the conclusion that something is wrong with the child and that a formal evaluation is needed to diagnose what is wrong. The underlying assumption is that diagnosing learning problems is like having a blood test to count your cholesterol. It is done all of the time. What have you got to lose? We can't do anything without your consent anyhow. The parents usually agree, seldom understanding that the school, by law, can force their children into placements of which they do not approve.

Some specialists are better diagnosticians than others. Some even make sense when they say that a child has a visual perception problem or some other version of nonsense. I used to do it. I was not as creative as some of the good ones, and I would weasel, using phrases, such as, "He is operating *like a child who has been diagnosed as having a learning disability*." Or "This profile is *similar to* profiles of others who have been diagnosed as LD." Or, "She is *eligible for placement* in a program for LD children." Or even, "He *may benefit* from placement in a program for children who are labeled as LD." In that way, I never had to say anyone had a learning disability.

Yet, my purpose was the same. The child was not doing well in the regular classroom. Many teachers can be downright mean when dealing with children whom they believe need special education and transferring the students may help. Sometimes the recommendation for special education placement is merely to gain respite from a poor or vindictive teacher. For example, my wife, who is a special education teacher, told me about a regular education teacher who expressed his concern about a particular student with the following, said in front of the entire class, "I don't know why you are in my class. You should be down the hall in Mrs. Finlan's class." That teacher certainly is not the type anyone would want a low achieving student to have.

When I was placing children in special classes, I rationalized what I was doing by claiming it was for the good of the student—to get him away from a vicious teacher, to a more relaxed curriculum, or to get her parents off her case. I was one of the thousands of experts who diagnosed children as having a problem that was child specific. One of the labels I used was LD, but other diagnosticians in other states might use a specific learning disability, dyslexia, dysgraphia, attention deficit disorder, perceptual disorder, dysfunctional memory, or a host of other terms. The result is still the same. The diagnosis becomes official—the disorder is within the child. A team then develops an individual educational program (IEP) that is, more often than not, a duplicate of most of the others that the special teacher has. She either copies it by hand or photocopies the pages of another student's IEP and insists that it is individual. No one, except for the naive parent, ever believes that it is anything like individual. The student is placed in a group for reading, math, spelling, social studies, or for other subjects in which he is found to be disabled.

The result of such treatment is a child placed into a trajectory of failure and self-doubt buttressed by the all-knowing adults able to call names and place blame on the child himself. There is no way out, for instruction is never provided on a par with what he would receive in regular classes. Schools teach fear—fear of failure, fear of mistakes, fear of being found out. It also teaches students to avoid putting forth effort, to become dependent on cues from the teacher, to play the games of learning, and to avoid real learning.

FIVE ASSUMPTIONS CONCERNING TESTING

Educational testing theorists caution that no conclusions about the results of tests can be made until at least five assumptions are met. The first assumption is *equal opportunity to learn.* When testing involves comparing responses to scores obtained by a sample or norm group, no conclusions can be reached regarding the individual's scores unless it can be assumed that the person being tested has had the same opportunity to learn the information being tested as the norm group. Of course, the problem with such inferences is that everyone has unique experiences. Variation in experiences equals variation in test scores. The point has been adequately demonstrated with the Black Intelligence Test for Children (BITCH Test). Black ghetto children outscored their white suburban counterparts by a goodly margin when asked such questions as When do the welfare checks come? or Who did Stagger Lee shoot? Do those questions measure intelligence? They measure intelligence just as much as questions like, What color is a ruby? measure intelligence. In both cases, opportunity to learn is what is being measured.

Although the assumption concerning equal opportunity seems obvious, it is violated constantly. During the early 1900s when immigrants were routinely tested at Ellis Island before being allowed to enter the United States, they were given several tests including IQ tests. Those who did well were allowed to enter the country; those who did poorly were often denied entrance. In fact, quotas were set up for immigration from each country based on how certain ethnic groups scored on IQ tests. Since the tests were administered in English, as you might expect, English-speaking people scored the highest and were afforded higher immigration quotas than people from countries where English was not spoken. Not surprisingly, people from western Europe, such as England, Ireland, and Wales, were more likely to score high and be admitted than people from Italy, Greece, Poland, or Yugoslavia.

What was really being tested by asking foreigners questions, such as What is an automobile? Their knowledge of English, of course. Foreigners who could not answer questions, such as What is your name? could not be expected to be so familiar with the language that they could tell what an automobile was.

By the same token, a nine-year-old child asked, What does quarantine mean? is being tested on his knowledge of the English language. A nine year old exposed to a great deal of language and reading is more apt to answer that question correctly that a student with limited experiences with language. Would you feel safe in asserting that the child with knowledge about the word *quarantine* is smarter than the child who did not know? Of course not. Quarantine is a word seldom used in everyday speech. Few nine year olds would have encountered it. However, psychologists and educationists make just such conclusions about children when they administer IQ tests. They seldom look at absenteeism, learning style, interest, socioeconomic status, or cultural background.

The second assumption concerning testing is just as important. *There must be equal motivation to do well.* If I ask a child to write answers to questions on a piece of paper, and she daydreams, I know nothing about whether the student can do the work. I only know that she did not do the work. What if another student assumes that he had better write something rather than just stare? Do I know whether he tried? No. So, when any test is given, either the assumption must be made that the motivation to do well is strong, or nothing can be concluded about the test results. Usually, the assumption is made that the motivation to do well was strong.

A third assumption is that *any child taking a test must be familiar with test-taking procedures and with tests.* If a child is taking a test for the first time, she will likely not do as well as if she has had experience with test taking procedures. That is why high school students practice taking the SAT so their scores will not be affected by inexperience with test taking. Imagine how little experience a five year old has with test taking and how infrequently he has been given an individually administered test. I am sure that to some students the task is overwhelming, yet kindergarten and preschool screening abounds in this country. If a child does not do well on the screening, his parents are told about what horrors await their child in school.

A fourth assumption regarding testing is that *all participants must be free of anxieties and emotional problems.* I once tested a girl who was an elective mute. That is, she was compelled for some unknown reason not to talk, especially to strangers. Her mother said she would go days at a time at home without talking. The girl was enrolled in a special education class, and I was required to reevaluate her placement. During the initial part of the testing, many times she did not speak even though it appeared that she wanted to speak. Eventually, I started putting my stopwatch in front of her and telling her to answer before the hand got to the ten-second mark. Using that procedure, she answered nearly ever question, usually blurting out an answer at the very last second. The testing situation itself was probably too stressful for her. She was certainly not free of anxieties, and her score probably was not accurate. She still scored in the retarded range and remained in special education, but I believe that she had much more potential than was ever measured by the IQ tests.

The fifth assumption regarding testing is that *the child must have no physical disabilities.* A child who is blind, deaf, or severely physically disabled obviously can't do well on most tests, but what of the child whose eyes do not focus congruently or the child who has a hearing loss in a limited range? He may not hear sounds of high frequency, but hears well enough that no one has ever diagnosed his disability. Is it fair to conclude that scores for students with those disabilities are accurate? Of course not. The point is, we do not know when we are testing such children.

THE REAL PURPOSE OF TESTING

The real purpose of testing is to draw conclusions regarding children's abilities and performance. The conclusions are what matters. Once the five assumptions have been met, and only then, can it be concluded that any scores from an evaluation might be accurate. As we test more and more children of preschool age and draw conclusions about them, how easy it would be to violate any one of the assumptions. A three-year-old child could hardly be considered to be free of anxieties when a stranger is probing her about who knows what. A three year old has had very limited experiences so how can we conclude equal opportunity to learn? Perhaps most important of all, how can a three year old be familiar with test-taking procedures? The fact of the matter is that very seldom can we be sure we are not violating some of the assumptions. Even with five, six, and seven year olds, we cannot be sure we are not violating assumptions of testing.

However, in my twenty plus years of working in the schools, I have never read a report that said the tests were inaccurate because assumptions were violated. Usually the reports mention what great rapport was established with the children, implying that covers all bases. Who could possibly know what is going on in the mind of a small child who has been whisked off to a small room to play some games with a stranger. Even meeting the five assumptions does not make the tests any better. The tests are not above suspicion. The most misused of all is the intelligence test.

TYPICAL IQ TESTS

The typical IQ test is composed of several sections of games, puzzles, and questions so that a general IQ score can be obtained rather than a score measuring only one ability, such as the ability to draw. The Wechsler Intelligence Scale for Children-Revised (WISC-R) is the test most often used in individual testing to measure intelligence. The test is composed of twelve subtests; six are designed to measure verbal IQ, and six are used to measure performance IQ. One of the verbal IQ subtests is the vocabulary section. A student is asked a series of increasingly difficult vocabulary words, such as What is a banana? What is a tractor? Or the question mentioned earlier, What does quarantine mean? The more questions answered correctly, the higher the IQ score. No one is born with that kind of knowledge. It is learned. What if you had only been in the United States for a short time, were raised by uneducated parents, or had a hearing problem? What are the chances of your having encountered the word *quarantine*? The chances are far less than if you were born in the United States, had normal hearing, and were raised by college-educated parents who read to you regularly, particularly if they read you stories about children quarantined for measles. Because you never learned the word *quarantine*, does it mean you are less intelligent than someone who learned the word at an early age? You cannot be judged regarding knowledge of that word or anything else, unless it can be confirmed you have had equal opportunity to learn. Remember, without equal opportunity to learn, we can draw no conclusions about a child's intelligence.

USE OF INTELLIGENCE TESTS

For a student to be labeled LD, he must be of at least average intelligence. No one wants to go out on a limb and say a student is of average intelligence without some measure. No one would want to make education decisions about a student based on biased or false information. The intelligence test seems like the only way of accurately determining intelligence. Give a child an intelligence test, so we know how smart she is. That kind of reasoning makes intelligence tests the main staple in the LD labeling process, the first step in getting a child in the LD door.

The problem with reliance on intelligence tests is that *there is no such thing as an intelligence test*. The tests that we call IQ tests are merely achievement tests. We test achievement and infer intelligence. An inference is a guess. You see, children are not born knowing the information on intelligence tests. They learn the information. Intelligence tests, by and large, are language or perception-oriented skills that are learned. Children answer questions and solve puzzles. Their scores on those tasks are compared to scores of similar aged children and a guess is made about intelligence.

A couple examples will suffice. Following are two questions. One is from a popular intelligence test. One is from an achievement test. Can you tell which is which?

1. Who discovered America?
2. Who discovered America for Spain?

The first question is from an IQ test. The second is from an achievement test. The questions are virtually identical. They are measuring the same knowledge with a slight twist, but one is measuring intelligence the other achievement. The second question is slightly different since it attempts to portray history more accurately, but we are left wondering how one question can measure intelligence while the other measures achievement. Of course, they cannot.

Not only do they not measure different traits, a more intelligent child might say that the Indians discovered America, but he would receive no credit for that insightful answer. If that answer is given, the examiner is told not to count it as correct, but to probe by asking Who sailed across the ocean and discovered America? Apparently, already living here doesn't count. Using that criterion, any immigrant who came by boat discovered America. An intelligent youngster would simply receive no credit for recognizing that the land was inhabited when Columbus landed.

Here are two more questions from the same two tests.

1. A boy had twelve newspapers and sold 5. How many did he have left?
2. A storekeeper had 12 pineapples. He sold five of them. Point...to the number of pineapples that he had left.

The first question calls for an oral answer; the second question gives four answers and the child is to recognize the correct answer by pointing, but the two questions are again measuring the same knowledge. The first is from an IQ test; the second from an achievement test.

Intelligence tests measure achievement (learning) and infer intelligence based upon how much information has been learned compared to other people of similar ages. Why similar ages? The assumption of equal opportunity to learn is the answer. It is assumed that all children born at the same time have had equal opportunity to learn. My niece was born three months prematurely and weighed 1 pound 13 ounces. On the day she was born, millions of other children were born, some probably weeks beyond due dates, 99.9 percent weighing far more than my niece. Not only that, she spent the first three months of her life in an incubator while those other children were being hugged, cuddled, and talked to. Is it reasonable to expect my niece to be compared to the children born on the same day she was? That is what will happen when she goes to school. Nearly every comparison will be with children who were born when she was born.

WHAT DO IQ TESTS MEASURE?

So-called IQ tests vary greatly in what they sample. A child may be asked to reconstruct a puzzle, define words, answer general information questions, or draw a human figure. It may appear at first blush that those are the things of which intelligence is composed. But without exception, those things are learned. Each test asks the person being tested to demonstrate some knowledge that other people who are believed to be like the person being tested demonstrated. If you can define words, draw a human figure with an appropriate number of body parts, or complete whatever tasks other people like you have done, you are declared to be average. If you can do more than others like you, you are said to be smart or above average. If you cannot answer the right questions, then you are declared to be below average or, even worse, retarded.

Intelligence, however, is susceptible to change. Arthur Whimbey has written *Intelligence Can Be Taught* in which it is argued that IQ scores can be changed, sometimes greatly, by instruction.[1] The makers of the Scholastic Aptitude Test (SAT) claimed for years that their test was not susceptible to instruction, but have recently conceded that preparation courses do influence scores. Intelligence is a learned ability and, just like most other abilities, can be improved with instruction and practice or can deteriorate with neglect.

THE CENTRAL QUESTION ABOUT IQ TESTS

The most significant question about IQ tests was posed by Sheldon White:

> The central question is whether the child's performance
> on the games, puzzles, and questions—those of the test
> and of the school—reflects some essence in the child so

significant that it should be considered to be merit, general ability, or promise to society.[2]

That is the important question. Does the combination of questions measure some essence? No one knows, yet such tests are used daily to measure thousands of students. There are few psychologists who do not have serious doubts about IQ tests. Intelligence (if there is any such thing) can hardly be reduced to a single, linear attribute any more than can sunsets or beauty. How about rating sunsets on a linear scale? Can you imagine a sunset quotient? Everyday in the newspaper you could read the SQ and know whether the sunset was average, above average, or severely above average. No matter how preposterous that seems, reducing a complex little understood concept, such as general intelligence, into a single number, like the marks on a tape measure, is far more preposterous.

There is no concept in psychology more criticized that the notion of a single intelligence. The idea of intelligence tests has been pooh-poohed for years. Some test makers have even sought to call their scores something besides intelligence. Jane Mercer chose School Functioning Level for the System of Multicultural Pluralistic Assessment; Dorothea McCarthy chose General Cognitive Index for the McCarthy Scales of Children's Abilities. However, even with a different name, the impression is still that those tests measure an immutable property. Despite the fact that IQ scores vary greatly, the general notion in education is that an IQ score is relatively stable. My personal experiences are different. I already mentioned the father who called me to have an IQ score removed from his son's file since it was 40 points different from his son's current score. Is that an isolated case? Not by a long shot.

A BOY NAMED GARY

Gary was an eleventh grader who was enrolled in special education classes for the mentally retarded since kindergarten. The state standards for special education, in the days prior to PL 94-142, called for the reevaluation every three years of a child's educational placement. It was under that requirement that I met and tested Gary.

In reviewing his records, I saw that the last time he was tested, in eighth grade, he had scored a full scale IQ score of 83. In

Pennsylvania 79 is the cut off for enrollment in classes for the mentally retarded. Gary's scores had been too high for him to continue in special education following the eight-grade evaluation. Despite that, he continued in special education for the next three years. Also of interest was the fact that his IQ scores had increased significantly every time he had been tested since that first test in kindergarten. His first IQ score was in the 50s—a level considered moderately to severely retarded. The psychologist said that Gary's scores were probably low because of a speech problem. As his speech improved so did his IQ scores. By eighth grade, his IQ score was in the 80s—low average ability. Apparently no one knew what to do for Gary when he tested out of special education, so they ignored the score and continued him in special education.

To test Gary's intelligence, I used the WISC-R which provides three IQ scores—a verbal score, a performance score, and a full scale score. What was surprising was that when I tested Gary, all three scores were above 80. But even more surprising, the performance score was 109, at the high end of average. His full scale IQ was in the 90s, dragged down by his relatively low verbal IQ score of 83.

The speech problem referred to in the kindergarten report had been a severe stuttering problem. Since the Stanford-Binet Intelligence Scale used for all of his previous evaluations has a strong verbal loading, I can only conclude that Gary was called retarded because he could not speak well enough to answer questions that he had known. His inability to answer was interpreted as retardation, and he had spent nearly eleven years of schooling in special education classes for the retarded.

The story does have a happy ending. Gary's special education teachers were perceptive, recognized his intelligence, and taught him at a higher level than the other special education students so that when I reevaluated him, he was able to be enrolled in regular education classes. The following year, he graduated with his class as a regular high school student. If I had not used the WISC-R with its performance scale, he might have again scored in the retarded range and been left in the retarded class. The beliefs about Gary's mental ability were set in kindergarten based on an inappropriate test. The psychologist covered herself by stating that the scores may have been low, but no one paid attention to the words in her reports. They looked at the scores and formed an opinion. The injustice was compounded by the triennial evaluations that continued to call him retarded.

A BOY NAMED BILLIE

I was fortunate to have been involved in rescuing Gary from an incorrect assignment, but I am not without blame when it comes to believing IQ tests. I tested another youngster a year or so later. I believed that I had established good rapport, for without that assumption, I could not call the results of the test reliable. The boy's name was Billy, and I believed that we got along wonderfully. The IQ score he obtained was low—a 73. That was consistent with his achievement test scores and the reports that his teacher had made about his school work. He was placed in an EMR class following the results of the testing. Almost immediately the EMR teacher began to bug me about Billy. He was far brighter that her other students. She didn't think he belonged. He was doing average work in many areas.

The following September, the teacher again began to tell me about Billy. He was too smart for her class. I agreed to retest him, and to my surprise, Billy scored nearly twenty points higher on the same IQ test less than six months later! It was the same test, the same psychologist, the same room, and, I believed, the same rapport. The only thing different was Billy's ability. His new IQ score was 92; he was of average intelligence. I could blame no other foolish psychologist. This time I was the fool for believing that IQ tests are accurate and for subjecting Billy and his family to the trauma of being labeled retarded.

A GIRL NAMED JULIE

Gary's and Billy's cases are not that unusual. Many times IQ scores are off by as much as forty or fifty points. Gary's score had increased, but sometimes IQ scores go down. I tested a girl named Julie who was supposed to be mentally gifted. Her second-grade teacher kept giving her extra work to challenge her. Julie's parents were concerned about Julie's well being since she came home nearly every day in tears because she could not cope with school and all the extra work. She was getting Cs and occasion Bs, but was still given extra work because she might be bored with the regular curriculum. You see, Julie had scored 143 on an IQ test. The highest score in the entire elementary school. When I administered the WISC—R, she scored 109. Instead of being disappointed, her parents were relieved and so was Julie. She was not a genius. She could relax and just be a kid again.

LAST JUDGMENT

The problem with the examples I have just cited is not the rarity of the problem but the underlying assumption—the IQ test gives a score that is somehow immutable and permanent. We were warned about such thinking in the 1920s by Walter Lippmann when IQ tests were beginning to take hold in the educational community. The citation is rather long, but exceedingly perceptive.

> If...the impression takes root that these tests really measure intelligence, that they constitute a sort of last judgment on the child's capacity, that they reveal "scientifically" his predestined ability, then it would be a thousand times better if all the intelligence testers and all their questionnaires were sunk without warning in the Sargasso Sea. One has only to read around in the literature of the subject,...., to see how easily the intelligence test can be turned into an engine of cruelty, how easily in the hands of blundering or prejudiced men it could turn into a method of stamping a permanent sense of inferiority upon the seal of a child.
>
> It is not possible, I think, to imagine a more contemptible proceeding than to confront a child with a set of puzzles, and after an hour's monkeying with them, proclaim to the child, or to his parents, that here is a C-individual. It would not only be a contemptible thing to do. It would be a crazy thing to do, because there is nothing in these tests to warrant a judgment of this kind. All that can be claimed for the tests is that they can be used to classify into a homogenous group the children whose capacities for school work are at the particular moment fairly similar. The intelligence test shows nothing as to why those capacities at any moment are what they are, and nothing as to the individual treatment which a temporarily retarded child may require.
>
> I do not say that the intelligence test is certain to be abused. I do mean to say it lends itself so easily to abuse that the temptation will be enormous...most of the more prominent testers have committed themselves to a dogma which must lead to just such abuse. They claim

not only that they are really measuring intelligence, but that intelligence is innate, hereditary, and predetermined. They believe that they are measuring the capacity of a human being for all time and that this capacity is fatally fixed by the child's heredity. Intelligence testing in the hands of men who hold this dogma could not but lead to an intellectual caste system in which the task of education had given way to the doctrine of predestination and infant damnation. If the intelligence test really measured the unchangeable hereditary capacity of human beings, as so many assert, it would inevitably evolve from an administrative convenience into a basis for hereditary caste.[3]

Unfortunately, Lippmann was more of a prophet that he had hoped to be. Tests are used routinely to "stamp a permanent sense of inferiority" upon children. The only difference is that we are now identifying millions of youngsters as being LD rather than mentally retarded, but we have, for sure, developed an educational caste system with the belief that the LD child is inferior and predestined.

NOTES

1. Whimbey, A. (1975). *Intelligence can be taught.* New York: Dutton.

2. White, S. H. (1977). Social implications of IQ. In Houts, P. L. (ed.), *The myth of measurability.* New York: Hart Publishing, p. 24.

3. Lippmann, W. (1976). The abuse of tests. In Bloch, N. J., & Dworkin, G. (Eds.) *The IQ controversy: Critical readings.* New York: Pantheon Books, p. 19-20.

7

Labeling

There are two groups of people in the world—those who divide people into two groups and those who don't.
Author Unknown

Like it or not, nearly every child who enters a public school will be labeled many times by many people. Some of the labels will be informal, and some will be formal. Some will be helpful or complimentary while some will be destructive and hurtful. Some will be applied by teachers, some by parents, some by other professionals, and some by other students.

Labeling is a fact of life. Whether we think it is good or bad does not matter; we cannot stop it, at least we cannot stop all of it. It is important to recognize that labeling unconsciously shapes the people who are labeled. Labeling is the result of a judgment and produces a social reaction. Whether the judgment is correct does not matter. Calling someone dumb or lazy produces someone who becomes dumb or lazy.

SPECIAL EDUCATION LABELS

Some of the most important labels in schools are those of special education, and the resulting social reactions are profound. Special education labels are labels of deviance and are applied to 17 percent of the entire school-aged population. Special education labels consist of such names as retarded, disabled, and disturbed—harsh words by any standard. The application of such labels is a matter of definition and degree. Deviance, like most other labels, is in the eye of the beholder. Labeling controls our thinking and perceptions.

An African tribe uses three words to describe the colors of the spectrum. Consequently, they see only those three colors. In their limited perception, red, orange, and yellow are the same color. In the same way, what we see is predicated on what our language allows us to see. The labels of language are labels of convenience. They allow us to look at things and behaviors in certain ways, but they also limit our thinking. Once we have divided the world into groups, we only see those groups. Missing out on the differences between yellow, orange, and red may not allow the African tribe to enjoy a sunset in the same way you or I would. Eskimos have thirty separate words for snow. We English speaking people have few such words since we do not need them. The ancient Greeks had one word which meant both past and future, a concept that is hard for us to understand, but they must have thought of the future in far different ways from what we do. Words really do limit our thinking.

LIMITING CHILDREN

By allowing our children to be categorized and pigeonholed, we limit them. Most of us have heard about students like Thomas Edison who did not do well in school but became highly successful as adults. Perhaps because they escaped the kinds of labels that current society applies, they were allowed to grow intellectually despite their difficulties in school. Few of our current younger generation will accomplish much if they are not successful in school because their opportunities will be limited by the labels applied to them while in school. They will be labeled as being at-risk, impaired, disadvantaged, disabled, retarded, or disturbed. Their parents will be counseled regarding lowered expectations. Some well-meaning guidance counselor will tell the parents of kindergartners about vocational technical programs at the high school, about working with their hands and how honorable those professions are, and how we will always need auto mechanics and roofers. Of course, those are not professions the counselors would want for their children, but they are sure that if the parents face reality, the child will be better off.

Lowered expectations brought about by labels applied by experts damn those children to lives as second-class citizens as soon as the adults in their lives buy into the labels. Look at the accomplishments of children whose parents went against the bureaucracy that was trying to label and limit their children. In many of those cases, the children excelled. Once Down syndrome children were immediately taken from parents and placed into institutions. Most of them were fed and cared for, but were not expected to accomplish much, if anything. As society became more enlightened, Down syndrome children stayed with their parents and attended public schools. The behaviors at the institutions had shaped our thinking about Down syndrome. Children with Down syndrome were viewed as low-functioning, trainable students. Parents who did not accept that fate have started keeping them home and have raised their children with hope. Now many Down syndrome children are educated in regular kindergartens and some even stay in regular classes for several years. One Down syndrome teenager has written a book about the day to day experiences of having Down Syndrome.[1] Another starred in the hit TV show, "Life Goes On." Thousands of others lead lives of virtual independence working at real jobs and maintaining their own living arrangements. We changed our thinking about Down syndrome and, not surprisingly, the achievements of those people have changed.

ARGUING FOR LIMITATIONS

Unfortunately, labels are easily accepted because they provide just enough truth to be dangerous. Some people see stocks as risky and never invest. They leave their money in banks. Others see the banks as risky and keep their money at home. Sam Snead, the famous golfer, even had a walk-in vault built in his home because he does not trust banks. Some people see airplanes as dangerous and never fly. Others claim air travel is the safest means of transportation available.

Whatever label we wish to apply to a situation can be applied, for we can always come up with some examples to prove our position. I can show you hundreds of examples of stocks that have gone down, banks that have failed, and airplanes that have crashed. I also can show you thousands of good stock investments, good banks, and safe flights, but once you have argued for a position, the label you apply controls your thinking. Your opinion will not change. You will continue to believe that stocks are risky, that flying is unsafe. By the labeling of events, you limit your possibilities. By labeling your children, you limit their futures. Labels promote misconceptions. *If you argue for your child's limitations, you will get them.*

We assign labels to people and situations all of the time, often unconsciously, so they can fit into the pigeonholes of our minds, but it makes a mess of what really exists. For example, the image we Americans have of car salespeople is not good. We see them as sleazy and deceitful, out to make a buck at any cost. The image is probably inaccurately applied to most of the auto industry, but it is a label that still controls our thinking. Armed with the knowledge of what most people think of salespeople, what do you do if you are in the business of selling cars? You change the image. "See your Cadillac consultant," Cadillac advertising entreats. Why did Cadillac choose the term consultant? To change our view of their sales staff. Cadillac saw the value of a positive label. A salesperson is out to make a buck, but a consultant seems to be working for you. Of course, do you honestly think their consultants would counsel you not to buy a Cadillac? Probably not, but a consultant sounds like someone who is on your side.

THE POWER OF LABELS

Labels force us to view the world as fixed and rational, filled with facts, truth, and clear-cut categories. When we label, we ignore the unusual, the human, the different, the unpredictableness of life. Trying to categorize human behavior may be helpful in the abstract but not in the specific.

Virtually no human characteristic is universal, and if it is not, why apply labels in the specific? Calling your son lazy is an easy way to describe what you think about his behavior at a certain time, but he has probably done many things that are not lazy behavior. By calling him lazy, you may create a lazy son. Finding different ways of looking at things is necessary. I read about an overweight woman who claimed she had no willpower, yet while visiting friends in Scandinavia, she flew to Rome to buy pasta to make an authentic Italian meal for her friends. Can you imagine grocery shopping outside the country by airplane? That woman had enough willpower to fly to Italy to buy pasta. She was not lacking in willpower, but by putting that label on herself, she limited her responses regarding her eating behaviors.

LD LABELING

Miscommunication is often the result of labeling. Just like the father who thought that giftedness was like being pregnant—either you are or you are not; most people view LD in like fashion: either you have it or you don't. Of course, that is sheer nonsense. LD symptoms may be mild or severe and cannot be segmented into clearly defined categories. Instead, a child becomes LD when a team of experts declares him to be LD, and he stops being LD when a team declares that he is not LD. Are those decisions based on clear-cut facts or opinion and feelings? Although the team gives the appearance of relying on facts and test scores, they ultimately rely on opinions and beliefs.

LABELS ARE ARBITRARY

One of the problems with dividing things into classes based on arbitrary schemes is that the divisions are unnatural. Decisions that have to be made around the edges are not neat and clean. Humans have conceived of numerous ways of dividing people into groups none of which is satisfactory. Look at the concept of race. When I was younger, I filled out numerous forms that asked my race. Three choices were given—Negro, Caucasian, or Oriental. Newer versions of those forms have more choices including Hispanic, Pacific Islander, American Indian, and Eskimo. Furthermore, Orientals now want to be called Asian, and Negro has changed to Black and more recently to African-American.

Hispanic is not even a race. Hispanic has to do with language. Many black-skinned people are Spanish-speaking, as are many white-skinned people. Also, many Native Americans seem to prefer being called American Indians after all. But what of Hottentots, Australian aborigines, and Alaskan Indians? Where do they fit in? Eskimos, for example, do not want to be confused with Alaskan Indians. They each must have separate categories on most forms. And what race is the person who has forebears of more than one race? Through how many generations do descendants remain African-American if they had only one black relative? That is the question Mark Twain was asking in *Puddinhead Jones.*

It all boils down to a mess. In fact, some sociologists claim that race is a myth. The authors of *Not in Our Genes: Biology, Ideology, and Human Nature* opine:

> the differences between major "racial" categories, no matter how defined, turn out to be small. Human "racial" differentiation is, indeed, only skin deep. Any use of

racial categories must take its justifications from some
other source than biology.[2]

Much the same is true of how we group children in
schools. Despite the fact that children are segregated and labeled
by so-called experts, biology is not the determining factor here
either. The experts themselves have little agreement on what
constitutes LD or who is eligible. Preconceived notions are what
determine the labels.

DISCREPANCY MODELS FAIL
AT IDENTIFYING LD STUDENTS

Usually students who are called LD are identified using a
discrepancy model fashioned by an expectancy formula, a
variation from grade level, or a standard score comparison. In
one study, such a discrepancy model was applied to eighty fourth
grade youngsters, forty of whom were labeled as LD, and forty of
whom were merely low achievers. Many LD subjects did not meet
the LD criteria established using federal guidelines and many low
achieving students could have been labeled LD using the same
federal guidelines.[3] There is no clear category of LD youngsters
who can be differentiated from other low achieving youngsters.

Chapter I disadvantaged programs and LD programs seem
to be serving students who are remarkably similar in many ways
and cannot be distinguished in any consistent way from each
other. Many of the students labeled as LD using discrepancy
methods cannot be differentiated from so-called garden variety
low achievers. In another study, performance measures of
reading, spelling, and written expression were administered
weekly over a five-week period to fifth-grade students. Approximately half of the students were labeled LD, and half were
merely low achievers. No meaningful differences between the
groups were found using norm-referenced measures.[4] One conclusion reached regarding ability-achievement discrepancies is
that:

> current reliance on unspecified degrees of discrepancy
> between ability and achievement is deceiving and may
> be ill- founded as a basis for a separate category of
> children to receive special education services.
> Professionals in the learning disabilities field should
> either recognize low achievement per se as a problem

and treat it in whomever it occurs, or conceptualize and define a category of children different from their low-achieving peers.[5]

If we view the identification of students who are eligible for services as the attempt to distinguish a distinct group of students who have certain characteristics, then labeling students as LD would merely be the assigning of the appropriate labels to students who exhibit serious difficulties in school. However, the professionals who are involved in identifying LD students, namely school psychologists and teachers, did no better at identifying LD students than did naive university students.[6] The obvious conclusion one can reach is that the so-called LD youngsters are not a unique group of students. In fact, it has been argued in the professional literature that a discrepancy definition does not produce a unique group of students, and the LD category has outlived it usefulness.[7]

CRITICISM OF CURRENT PRACTICE

What seems to be the most important consideration in determining whether a child is LD? The decision by a teacher to refer students for evaluation for special education is the primary factor. There are many problems with the current system as it attempts to categorize children with a team of professionals. Among the problems with such team decisions are lack of teacher participation, use of nonvalid diagnostic instruments, and the tendency to base placement decisions on a limited amount of relevant data. It was concluded in one study that the definitions of LD are broad enough to include the majority of normal children, so that *most children who are referred are declared eligible for services*.[8] After that, the decisions have little to do with the data collected since the data does not distinguish a separate group of students.

One researcher has called for the abandonment of the discrepancy model in determining LD primarily because the IQ test is seen as being irrelevant.[9] The concept of a discrepancy is poorly defined and based on constructs and criteria that are questionable at best. The LD field has also been accused of having a propensity for latching onto concepts that are tenuous and controversial.

> The decision to base the definition of a reading disability on a discrepancy with measured IQ is still nothing short of astounding. Certainly one would be hard pressed to find a concept more controversial than intelligence in all of psychology. [10]

Neither is there any reason to seek a discrepancy in only one direction. Reading is generally considered discrepant from IQ rather than IQ from reading, but there are effects running in both directions. The concept of discrepancy itself is also ludicrous. Look at a baseball player who is an excellent fielder but can't hit. Is his hitting discrepant from his fielding, or vice versa? Based on his tremendous fielding, his hand-eye coordination (visual motor integration) must be exceptional, yet based on his hitting ability his hand-eye coordination must be poor. Which ability is discrepant from the other? Also, many exceptional hitters cannot field. In which direction is the discrepancy in those cases?

THE HARSH REALITY OF LABELS

In the world of closed minds, no one is happier than the bureaucrats who label children and get parents to sign forms consenting to the labels. Parents are told that LD classes are for average to above average students; that the classes provide individual instruction; that their children are only slow in reading or in some other academic area. Many of the bureaucrats honestly believe what they are saying and ignore the harsh realities of the real world.

And, the realities are harsh. Imagine waking up one morning and finding your fourteen-year-old son's name in the paper listed as retarded when you were told he was learning disabled? When you were promised by experts that he was of average intelligence? When you were told that he only had a problem in reading? Well, that is what happened to the father of a boy in the Allentown, Pennsylvania, area. In the June 8, 1991, edition of the *Allentown Morning Call*, the father described his son as an average kid—except for reading. "He's only slow in reading, that's all I know." That is probably what the bureaucrats told him to get him to agree to the special education placement, yet listed in a previous edition of the newspaper were the names of mentally retarded athletes competing in the local Special Olympics. Included on the list was the boy in question. The father was incensed. Why was his son called retarded and why was it published in the newspaper?

One of the boy's teachers said that four of the students included on the list were not mentally retarded but instead have relatively serious learning disabilities. She went on to explain, "Even though the intelligence is there the connections between senses and the brain are not working in some way." What does some nonsense about connections between the senses and the brain have to do with why the boy's name was published in the newspaper with a list of retarded students? And did she mean all of the senses were faulty—like taste and touch—or did she just mean vision and hearing? Or did she mean only the visual perception of print? Remember, the father said the boy was average except for reading. Do you suppose his brain connections are only messed up when they are connecting the recognition of squiggles on paper? Furthermore, the teacher never explained where exactly the intelligence was, but it certainly was treated as if it were a thing.

More important, a fourteen-year-old boy, who was probably at the most sensitive age regarding the development of his self-image, was listed in a public newspaper (a violation of federal confidentiality laws) as being retarded and was allowed (or forced) to attend a Special Olympics track meet designed only for the retarded. Where is the outrage? Certainly there was none on the teacher's part. How about the state director of the Special Olympics? He defended the Special Olympics by saying:

> This is some backlash to labeling.... They are saying they don't want their children to have that label.... But clearly there must be some cognitive delay here, or they would not be eligible to compete. They are performing academically below acceptable, normal standards. I think that's a pretty fair statement.

What does "performing below acceptable, normal standards" have to do with retardation? Where is the concern for the boy's esteem? Why would the state director assume that "performing below acceptable, normal standards" makes one retarded? Because that is what he and millions of others really believe. Why were the LD students included in an event designed only for the retarded? Because the bureaucrats and teachers really believe that they are all the same—retarded. Regardless of the con game used to convince the parents to place their children in special education, many people believe LD is just a fancy name for retarded.

Much of the problem with ideas, such as LD, has to do with the fuzzy thinking employed to arrive at the conclusions. Fuzzy thinking is the result of using fuzzy words that often do not mean much of anything but what the user wishes. George Orwell in his essay "Politics and the English Language" writes, "A mass of Latin words falls upon the facts like soft snow, blurring the outlines and covering up all the details." [11] LD's jargon blurs the outlines and covers the details.

Someone who is LD in one school district in New York may not be LD in Kansas, Colorado, or even in another school district in New York. The labelers themselves, the special education professionals trained in the methods of special education and the educational requirements are victims of their own social experiences and beliefs which produce severely different views depending on those experiences and beliefs. A principal who has little belief in the value of self-contained classes may not allow many students to be labeled as LD if they must be placed in such programs. Another principal who believes that special education teachers are specially trained may place far more students into the same programs. Someone who believes that children are victims of their environments may place far more students in LD than someone who believes in the ability of all students.

THE MAKING OF AN LD STUDENT

Students given any label, but particularly a label of deviance sanctioned by the state and by the professional community, no longer are perceived without benefit of the typing that comes from such a label. Other people's reactions to them are heavily influenced by the label, and the person becomes a virtual deviant by the process of the label. Josh was the product of just such labeling. He was a marginal student who was eventually labeled LD in seventh grade following several testings in elementary school where he did not qualify for LD. How did he suddenly become LD? By declaration of a team of experts, probably the same experts who would not label him as LD on at least three previous occasions in elementary school. Instead, they waited until his chronological age outpaced his achievement scores so he could be called LD.

Josh became LD in junior high based on an average IQ score and on one discrepant score on a spelling test. All of his other achievement scores were within expectations, including math and reading, yet, in a few short months, he was enrolled in the LD program for all academic subjects. Once his other teachers knew he was LD for part of the day, they pushed to get him in LD all day. Despite a qualifying score only on a spelling test (a test which should never have been used for placement, only for screening), he became a virtual LD in a few short weeks. Josh had been evaluated for LD placement at least four times in his seven years of schooling, yet only had one achievement score on a spelling test discrepant from expectancy. Regardless, he became LD for all subjects once the door was opened. Josh had no voice. His parents trusted the experts, and Josh was sent to a second-class education.

We view ourselves through the eyes of others, particularly when other people's view is powerful or of long enough duration. That is what happened to Josh. Other people's views were so powerful, that he succumbed. Josh may have had difficulty spelling, but once the label of LD was bestowed upon him, he became more than a person who did not spell well. He became disabled in the eyes of all who dealt with him. He became more to be pitied than helped.

THE LD LABEL IS THE RESULT
OF THE RULES APPLIED

Unfortunately, the LD label is more the result of the rules applied to the person than the behaviors of the person observed. The effect of a deviant label is the result of an interaction between the person labeled and the people doing the labeling. Once a student is labeled, everyone starts thinking of the student as different. Compounding the problem is the belief that nearly any behavior which is different is a symptom of LD. A traumatic birth, an interest in the occult, hard rock music, too much TV or Nintendo, not looking people in the eye, sneezing bouts, getting tatoos, taking drugs, or even armed robbery. Parents can confirm the label on a daily basis by hundreds of little mannerisms or characteristics that other parents would ignore. The parents start saying that they always knew he was different.

Teachers also respond differently. They no longer expect work to be completed (after all, not completing work is a characteristic of being LD), they do not expect the student to pay attention (attention deficit disorder), and they do not expect the student to learn (learning disabled, remember).

More than anything, however, the student responds differently. He no longer has to learn. His ability to avoid work has paid off. All of the adults in his life no longer require him to work. At least not in any real sense. The LD teacher may give him work to do, but it will be easy and if he doesn't do it, well, no matter. There will be more time and more days to learn that 2 X 6 = 12. If he doesn't learn it, we'll give him a calculator. Learning is unnecessary anyhow. The big difference is that can't is confused with won't. Karen Zelan argues in *The Risks of Knowing* that many so-called LD youngsters are in reality deliberate non-learners. For a variety of reasons, most involving personal defenses, some children deliberately choose not to learn. Educators err when they blame nonlearning on the child's capacity instead of her will and interaction with this environment.[12]

In current practice, the applying of the LD label is not a result of the behaviors of the student, it is a result of the rules and procedures applied to the behaviors by others that makes the person deviant. Whether a person is LD depends upon people's reactions to the behaviors. For example, in the rural area in which I work, teachers and administrators are far more concerned with what are only mildly troublesome behaviors than they would be in inner-city schools. Smoking in the lavatory is a major offense, so is talking back to a teacher, and so on. In the city school, knives, guns, and drugs are issues of deviance. A child is more apt to be called LD in our rural area because of talking back to a teacher than she would be in an urban school.

Much of the LD labeling is seen as enlightenment and the children are viewed as being lucky. If they lived somewhere else or had been born earlier, their problems would not have been diagnosed and the child would have suffered the consequences. The fact that special education is a mandated service also allows the system to label and make changes in a person's behavior. Common sense might not prevail. Instead, professionals think they don't have a choice. If the student meets criteria, they think they must enroll him.

NOTES

1. Hunt, N. (1967). *The world of Nigel Hunt; The diary of a mongoloid youth.* New York: Garrett Publications.

2. Lewontin, R. C., Ross, S. P. R., & Kamin, L. J. (1984). *Not in our genes: Biology, ideology, and human nature.* New York: Pantheon.

3. Ysseldyke, J. E., Algozzine, B., Shinn, M. R., & McGue, M. (1982). Similarities and differences between low achievers and students classified as learning disabled. *Journal of Special Education,* 16, 73-85.

4. Shinn, M. R., Ysseldyke, J. E., Deno, S. L., & Tindal, G. A. (1986). *Journal of Learning Disabilities*, 19(9), 545-552.

5. Algozzine, B., & Ysseldyke, J. E. (1983). Learning disabilities as a subset of school failure: The oversophistication of a concept. *Exceptional Children*, 50(3), p. 245-6.

6. Epps, S., Ysseldyke, J. E., & McGue, M. (1984). "I know one when I see one": Differentiating LD and non-LD students. *Learning Disability Quarterly*, 7(1), 89-101.

7. Algozzine, B. (1985). Low achiever differentiation: Where's the beef? *Exceptional Children*, 52(1), 72-75.

8. Algozzine, B., & Ysseldyke, J. E. (1983). Learning disabilities as a subset of school failure: The oversophistication of a concept. *Exceptional Children*, 50(3), 242-246.

9. Siegel, J. (1989). Is IQ necessary in the identification of LD? *Journal of Learning Disabilities*, 22(8), 487-492.

10. Stanovich, K. E. (1989). Has the learning disabilities field lost its intelligence? *Journal of Learning Disabilities*, 22(8), p. 487.

11. Orwell, G. (1968). Politics and the english language. In *The collected essays, journalism, and letters of George Orwell. Volume IV In front of your nose 1945-50.* London: Secher & Warburg.

12. Zelan, K. (1991). *The risks of knowing.* New York: Plenum.

8

Self-Fulfilling Prophecies

Decide not rashly. The decision made can never be recalled.
Longfellow

It is generally accepted that the prediction of a certain outcome can itself help produce that very outcome. Saying a student is lazy, dumb, or a troublemaker can help influence his behavior to become or to remain that way. Once a label is applied or a name is called, it may be too late to recall it. I evaluated a girl named Mandy who was repeating kindergarten. The teacher who made the referral, among other things wrote that, "Mandy cannot even count to ten."

Well, whenever I encounter something as definitive as cannot applied to a child, the first thing I attempt to do is to disprove the assertion. While working with Mandy, I had her recite, "one little, two little, three little Indians" until she said it with ease. She counted pencils, tiles on the floor, and her fingers until she counted to ten with no effort. I then told her that she had learned to count to ten. Mandy responded in a surprising manner. She exclaimed that she hadn't really learned to count to ten; that she would never learn to count to ten because her mother had told her she couldn't. She began to make mistakes and no longer could repeat "Ten Little Indians" without error.

I imagined what must have occurred at home when Mandy was younger. Her mother, who had at some point become completely frustrated with Mandy's seeming inability to count to ten, had probably exclaimed, "You'll never learn to count to ten." The mother probably stopped trying to teach her, also. Having been told by her mother that she would never learn to count to ten, Mandy stopped trying to learn. Unconsciously, she wanted to prove her mother was right. That is the self-fulfilling prophecy at work. Damning children with such comments is tantamount to condemning them to lives of failure.

The expectations that others have for us heavily influence our own expectations as well. Just as Mandy believed that she was incapable of learning a simple task like counting to ten, other students believe limits that have been placed by others. Fortunately, positive comments can also provide self-fulfilling prophecies.

How the School Manufactures "Misfits" by Delos Kelly describes the influences of self-fulfilling prophecies and how schools contribute to them. Kelly asserts that students who pass through schools acquire reputations that precede them. Kelly quotes a study from 1967 which in part states:

> All too often the teachers' lounge or coffee room is the burying ground for students' success chances, as teachers openly inform each other about students "to watch out for," or confirm each other's negative assessments of so and so's attitude or conduct.[1]

A BOY NAMED JAKE

Those reputations shape the way in which others in the schools treat the students. A boy named Jake was in his third try at the seventh grade. (Allowing a student to stay in seventh grade for three years tells a lot about the school but that is another discussion.) Since Jake had been in seventh grade for so long, was assigned to an LD class, seldom did his homework, and got into a lot of minor scrapes—such as smoking in the lavatory—he had a reputation which was well known. As part of his mainstreaming, he was assigned to a regular classroom for study hall where he invariably got into trouble. Just as students get reputations, so do teachers. The study hall teacher had a reputation for being unable to control the behaviors of her students, and the students acted accordingly. Most misbehaved by talking out loud, answering back, and being generally disruptive. Yet, the only student to have been sent to the office repeatedly was Jake, the three time seventh grader. Why was that?

If the teacher were to send students to the office who did not have reputations for misbehavior, the teacher's ability as a disciplinarian would be questioned by the principal. Instead, she sought to set an example by sending Jake, who everyone knows is trouble, to the office. Jake was talkative in study hall just as the other students were. The teacher threatened all of the students and finally sent Jake to the office to set an example for the other students. At any one time, most of the other students could be doing the same things Jake was doing, but Jake was the student most likely to misbehave so he was chosen to be sent to the office. And so it goes. Expectations control the outcomes.

ONCE REPUTATIONS ARE ESTABLISHED

Once reputations or beliefs about students are set, teachers may unwittingly reinforce those behaviors or beliefs. Teachers tend to avoid contact with students who have reputations as troublemakers or poor students. If a formal label, such as LD, is applied, many teachers claim that they are not trained to deal with that type of student, or they accept her only for study halls, class trips, group work, and the like. Not only do they reinforce their perceptions of LD and of the particular student, they avoid opportunities to change their perceptions.

In *How the School Manufactures "Misfits"*, Kelly tells of a teacher who saw a student sitting in the school office. The teacher assumed that the boy must be in trouble. The next day the teacher commented in front of the student's friends regarding the trouble the student must be in. The boy got smart with the teacher, reinforcing the teacher's belief that the student was a troublemaker, yet the boy was in the office only to change his schedule. If the teacher had no established beliefs about the boy's conduct in school, the teacher would never have approached the student in front of his friends and humiliated him. The student, in turn, would never have acted smart and there would have been no negative encounter. The teacher's beliefs about the student got in the way of fair treatment.

On the other hand, a good student walking in the hall without a hallway pass may be joked with by a teacher while a troublemaker may be hassled. Kelly concludes, "When good students deviate, we assume their behavior is either accidental or justified by the circumstances. It is hard to impute malicious intent to a basically good person."[2]

Deviance, LD being just one example, is not something someone does or is born with. It is a status conferred upon the student by the school. Unfortunately, it changes the manner in which the students are dealt with. Missing ten spelling words on a test may be a sign of not studying, but if the student is LD, more often than not, it is assumed that he can do no better. Expectations of underachievement become self-fulfilling prophecies.

A GIRL NAMED JANET

Once a student is called LD, it is difficult to change her image. Every significant adult in her life will have certain notions about her because of the LD label. A girl I met while I was a school psychologist provides an excellent example. When I encountered Janet, she was an attractive seventeen year old with long dark hair, milk white skin, and dark eyes. I was at first surprised that a girl who looked like her was being referred for evaluation, perhaps attesting to my own prejudices.

However, I soon discovered that Janet was a girl who had virtually no ability to deal with numbers because she had not been required to take math from early in grade school. She had attended a campus school at a local university which promoted the open classroom concept and the idea of student choice in curriculum. Janet was a good artist and elected to spend much of her time drawing, a decision the school fully supported. Janet was not good at math and elected not to take math classes, again a decision the school supported. Janet, while in the primary grades, was allowed to make those decisions. You can imagine what little math knowledge she had at age seventeen, having opted out of formal math instruction when she was six or seven. Despite an IQ score in the average range, Janet could not tell time, could not read a calendar, could not make change for a dollar, and refused to handle money of any kind. Janet, who loved ice cream, would not buy herself an ice cream cone for fear of being embarrassed if given the wrong change. Instead, Janet's mother made all of Janet's purchases.

There was no reason that Janet could not count change or read the face of a clock, other than she had never learned to do those things. She had never learned since she had opted out of the math program in second grade in a school that allowed choice in the curriculum. The school's progressive thinking was "Why should we make Janet take math which she doesn't like when she wants to spent time drawing, which she does like?" The answer was all too obvious at age seventeen. Janet was so fearful of numbers, having avoided them for so many years, she had become a handicapped adult. When the campus school was closed,

Janet had to enroll in the public schools. To meet the graduation requirements of the public schools, Janet had to have high school mathematics courses. Her choices were algebra, geometry, trigonometry, and calculus, yet she was unable to add double-digit numbers. Janet became LD by default.

THE NEED TO LEARN

Children are born with the need to learn. Almost immediately they begin learning all sorts of things. They learn the powerful force of cause and effect, primarily through the power of crying. A child can get attention almost immediately after birth with a few cries. As the parents become more accustomed to the newborn, they become more selective in their response to tears. Parents who do not become selective eventually have babies who cannot sleep without the constant comforting of the parents. Most sleep disturbances are learned behaviors, as are most other atypical behaviors.

Children continue to learn at a seemingly astronomical rate as they develop. I am constantly amazed by my little nieces and nephew and the level of their understanding. One nephew, who was not even three at the time, was ordered by his mother to either pick up his toys from the living room or get a spanking. He did not pick up the toys and was spanked. Then, instead of picking up the toys, he promptly started walking upstairs whereupon his mother asked why he was leaving. His response? "I got spanked, so I don't have to pick up my toys."

Of course, his mother, while not intentionally offering a choice, had, in fact, offered a choice, "Are you going to pick up your toys, or do you want to get spanked?" For a two year old to notice the subtlety and to act upon it shows the type of learning that has already taken place at age two.

READING IS EASY

By the time a child is six or seven and has begun reading instruction, he or she can tackle many, many things that are quite difficult—playing the violin, hitting a baseball, preparing microwave meals, running a VCR, playing Nintendo, to name just a few. To think that some of those same children are unable to learn to read is preposterous. Reading is not all that difficult. It is learning a few sounds and letter patterns to decode passages.

Just as nearly everyone learns to talk, nearly everyone can learn to read. The fact that some don't learn to read as well as we would like them to has allowed adults to ponder what is wrong with the children instead of what is wrong with the system used to teach them to read. I have never personally encountered a child with an IQ of more than 70 who cannot read. (Most students with an IQ of more than 50 can read.) Even the most disabled of readers can decode some words. A sixteen-year-old student reading at a middle-first-grade level may have an extreme problem, but even he is reading. The words may be one syllable words, but he can identify them. The same neurological system that allows him to read one syllable words will allow him to read two syllable words, and so on. Once the ability to read is established, even at a minimal level, refining the skill is all that is needed. What usually happens is that poor readers avoid reading and are allowed to. No one can improve skills without practice. Reading is no different.

William James, the psychologist, has been credited with the concept of finding one white crow as the only evidence needed to prove that not all crows are black.[3] Finding only a few words that can be read by an LD youngster should be the white crow needed to prove that the child can read. Once it has been shown that the student can read, all the theories about brain damage, auditory processing problems, visual processing problems, and the like should be dismissed. The ability to read a few words should be proof of reading and should remove any question of faulty wiring in the brain. *The task then becomes one of refining a skill rather than believing no skill exists.* However, the pervasive belief is that the child is at fault. Almost never is the system or the teacher considered to be at fault. Therefore, little effort is put into actual reading instruction. Once it is assumed, either formally or informally, that a child cannot read, little real effort goes into instruction or expectations for achievement. What is the use?

It is the child's behavior or genetics, his family or his heritage, it is what the child brings to school that is at fault. That belief has produced the concept of LD and that belief must be changed.

A GRANDMOTHER TO TEACH READING

The introduction to *Why Johnny Still Can't Read* was written by Mary Burkhardt who was director of reading in the Rochester (New York) City Schools. Burkhardt's introduction begins by avowing that she was "taught" to be a reading failure by *the method used to teach her to read* (emphasis added)—the so-called look-say method. Burkhardt explains, "I not only know about the reading problem in our schools, but I am well aware of how it feels to be labeled a reading failure. Feeling is a lot more acute than just knowing!"[4]

Burkhardt recounts how after years of reading failure, her grandmother sat her down night after night and taught her to sound out words using phonics. Eventually, Burkhardt became a good reader and wished to become a reading teacher when she entered college. After many years in the Rochester schools as a teacher and reading director, Burkhardt concluded

> I am convinced, without a doubt, that a superior program taught by well-trained teachers enables *all* children to learn to read.... The child who is truly reading disabled (dyslexic) is very rare. When children are taught to read in a structured, teacher-directed instructional program, they read. When this is not done, many children experience difficulty and are then mislabeled as dyslexic, an excuse.[5]

Burkhardt goes on to talk about the success of phonics-first programs in Rochester schools by saying:

> Throughout this country, our teachers desperately need to take the best reading programs into the classrooms with them. Then they will be able to eliminate the mystery of reading and ensure that children become independent readers. Distinguished researchers...have completed numerous research studies that document exactly what Rochester's students have demonstrated. One program is *not* as good as another.[6]

Any child who is having difficulty reading needs a grandmother like Burkhardt's who will take the time to teach letter sounds and keep at it until the child can read. Too often the child is written off instead of taught.

CHILDREN VALUE WHAT
THEY LEARN TO VALUE

What children learn to value helps shape their achievement. Children who value music may become interested in playing an instrument at an early age. If they are encouraged, their parents may buy an instrument and pay for lessons until they are a proficient. Other children become interested in other things—sports, flying airplanes, dancing, horseback riding, or playing chess. Most seek their parents' attention and approval and will do what it takes to obtain them.

Some children value other things, such as safety and are unwilling to take risks that might embarrass or harm their egos. Some of those children may become poor readers since they will not risk failure at any task. A student may be much more willing to have people accuse him of being lazy than of being stupid. Thus, when a teacher is about to pull her hair out because a child will not even try, she should be reminded of the child's need to protect his ego. Badgering him to "just try it," "sound it out," "at least say something" can be the result of frustration on the teacher's part, but knowing that it is valuable to a child not to be embarrassed or humiliated may help change the view and the approach the teacher uses to encourage reading.

DEFINITIONS & NAME CALLING

The definition of normal should be expanded rather than the definition of abnormal. People like to call names, and calling someone LD is certainly name calling. In fact, when I was employed as a school psychologist, I was often asked to speak at parent teacher meetings and for civil groups. I always referred to myself as the worst name caller in the county since I was the man who went from school to school and labeled children as LD or retarded or emotionally disturbed. Talk about a heavy burden. I had a great deal of difficulty doing it and only did it after great thought and concern.

Labeling someone a certain way helps produce whatever label has been applied. Parents who think they are being cute when they tell their two year old, "You're bad" or "You're so bad." should not be surprised when their child does something which is bad. Neither should we be surprised when educators, in their official capacities, declare students cannot learn to read, and the students oblige by not learning to read.

NOTES

1. Kelly, D. H. (1978). *How the school manufactures "misfits."* South Pasadena, CA: Newcall, p. 16.

2. Ibid., p. 33.

3. Ross, A. O. (1976). *Psychological aspects of learning disabilities & reading disorders.* New York: McGraw-Hill, p. 75.

4. Burkhardt, M. (1981). Introduction. In Flesch, R. *Why Johnny still can't read.* New York: Harper & Row., p. xiii.

5. Ibid., p. xx.

6. Ibid., p. xx.

9

Special Education

There are only two things wrong with most special education...it isn't special and it isn't education.
Alice Metzner

What seems obvious is not always correct; what is correct is not always obvious. Special education is no exception. It seems to make sense that identifying children having difficulty in regular classes and providing them with a separate education would be wise and humane. It would be unfair to frustrate children with academic demands they cannot meet. That is the current, seemingly informed, point of view in education. The thinking goes, "The only people opposed to special education are heartless humans who don't want anything for the good of the people because it might cost taxpayer dollars. Those of us who are informed could not possibly be opposed to providing additional help to handicapped children." Regardless, some people are still opposed to providing help to so-called handicapped children, especially if those children are not truly handicapped. What if their so-called handicap cannot be demonstrated except through inference? What if they are declared to be handicapped based on poor school performance? That is precisely what has occurred with LD students. Blind students cannot see; deaf students cannot hear; even mentally retarded students have difficulty solving mental puzzles, but LD students have no measurable problem except underachievement. It is assumed that some hidden disability keeps them from average school performance. No one ever expects them to learn at an average rate once they have been declared to be LD. They are given what is called a special education. Perhaps, it would be okay to label children as handicapped if they were receiving the kind of education which was helping them, but that is not the case.

As people become more informed concerning special education, the more likely they are to criticize it. In fact, some of the giants in special education back in the 1960s declared that special education was a failure. Of course, they did not use those words. Educators seldom are that forthright in their appraisals. However, one such researcher, Lloyd Dunn, said that, " a large portion of so-called special education in its present form is obsolete and unjustifiable."[1] He went on to say that students who were eligible for special education, but who had never been placed in special education, were as well off academically, or perhaps even better off, than if they had been placed in special education classes. According to Dunn and others, special education just didn't help. It may even have hurt many students. The researchers began calling for the altering of special education programs. They pushed for more integration and less isolation. Since the researchers were respected leaders in the special education field, they helped turn public sentiment away from self-contained classes for the mildly handicapped. Their views set the stage for the adoption of the concept of mainstreaming set forth in PL 94-142.

MAINSTREAMING AND THE REGULAR EDUCATION INITIATIVE

Despite the fact that the concept of mainstreaming was included in PL 94-142 (the word itself was never mentioned), mainstreaming was more of a buzz word than an actuality. Special education was and still is isolationistic. A movement in special education during the 1980s, often referred to as the regular education initiative (REI), has been the rebirth of the notion of effective mainstreaming based on the least restrictive environment (LRE) model required by PL 94-142 and the development of proposals to accomplish such ends. Even though nearly all LD students are mainstreamed part of the day, the current system of special education, according to the REI proponents, is "flawed, discriminatory, programmatically ineffective, and cost inefficient."[2] Instead of keeping the current system, some REI proponents are calling for a dissolution of the current dual system of special and regular education to be replaced by a more effective system for all students.[3] The proposal for the development of a single system has promoted much debate. Nobody wants handicapped students in their classes. They are too much trouble.

The REI proponents point to efficacy studies regarding special education when calling for restructuring. Studies of the effectiveness of special education have been unable to show significant differences in special education programs even with smaller class size and specially trained teachers. A look at those studies may be helpful in understanding the push toward mainstreaming.

GENERAL SPECIAL EDUCATION
EFFICACY STUDIES

An analysis of fifty studies regarding special education effectiveness suggested that students were no worse off and may have been better off academically if they had never been placed in special education classes to begin with, despite the higher costs and lower teacher-pupil ratios associated with special classes. The researchers, Conrad Carlberg and Kenneth Kavale, concluded that "special class placement is an inferior alternative to regular class placement in benefiting children removed from the educational mainstream."[4] The authors caution that differences may be the result of self-fulling prophecies and that absolute judgment regarding efficacy should be withheld. Who cares why the classes are failing? They are far more expensive and don't seem to help the very students they are designed to help.

One exception, according to Carlberg and Kavale, was that special education programs may have benefited behaviorally disordered and LD children. A note of caution should be observed in interpreting that conclusion regarding the LD children. Carlberg and Kavale stated that approximately 860 studies were identified for possible inclusion in their analysis. Of the 860, only fifty met their criteria for inclusion. Of those fifty studies only two of the studies listed in their bibliography mentioned LD students. Of those two studies, only one showed a positive effect for special education placement. Thus, the Conrad and Kavale's conclusions regarding LD were based on one out of a possible 860 studies. Additionally, that particular study[5] was criticized by other researchers for a poor selection of dependent variables and for some of the conclusions it reached. Furthermore, in 1988 when Kenneth Kavale again looked at the results of the effectiveness of LD programs, he was far less optimistic and concluded that, "it appears that learning disability symptoms, particularly in academic and behavioral areas, are long-standing and possibly not as amenable to treatment as previously believed."[6] Another way of saying that is that LD programs, as they are currently structured, do not work.

In another major study of the effectiveness of special education programs, the authors concluded that, "Little evidence exists supporting the efficacy of special education or the development of differential programs as a result of the assessment-placement process."[7] After an exhaustive search of the literature, the authors called for a redirection of focus saying that, "Effort must be directed at the development of systems for measuring the implementation of instruction and the consequent evaluation of effects."[8] According to the authors, the issue of effectiveness is one of instruction more than one of placement. That is, *we should be more concerned with how we are teaching than with where we are placing children*, yet in the LD literature, emphasis has always been on the label and the eligibility criteria.

LD RESEARCH

Very few studies have been conducted regarding the benefits of placement options solely for LD students. Most studies include MR and behaviorally disordered children as well as LD. However, some indications of benefit for mainstreaming have been found. Margaret Wang and Edward Baker conducted a meta-analysis of studies measuring the effects of mainstreaming.[9] Of 264 studies considered, 11 met acceptable criteria for inclusion. The results indicated a positive effect for mainstreaming over self-contained classes.

In another study of the effects of placement, comparison of pre- and post test scores on reading, math, and language subtests of an individually administered achievement test indicated no significant differences for second to fifth-grade students with LD in integrated classrooms and resource rooms.[10] Since integrated classrooms are more cost effective and achieve similar results, it could be argued that labeling students as LD and placing them in separate classes is too costly an enterprise for the benefits received, or it could also be argued that teaching in the separate classes has not been effective.

One author argued that the current belief system of special education shunts into special education programs too many children whose needs could be met in regular classrooms. He maintained that the current practices encourage a system that is excessively costly and that many of the currently identified handicapped could be educated in *a general education system that gave greater attention to individual needs.*[11]

Most of the current research indicates that special education as an alternative placement has generally failed to demonstrate effectiveness of programs, especially self-contained programs, for mildly handicapped children. This does not mean that there is no benefit for some students or in some settings since good teachers can make a difference no matter what. However, allowing large numbers of low-achieving students to be placed in special education classes by labeling them as handicapped may be detrimental.

First of all, there is no clear evidence of such an ailment as learning disabilities. Labeling children as such is deceit of the highest order. Second, placing children so labeled into special classes with teachers who are absolutely overloaded is irresponsible. LD teachers have an average of twenty-one students from three or more grade levels and must help those students in several subjects. Talk to any LD teacher; he or she will tell you that their task is nearly impossible.

A BOY NAMED JOEY

On the first day Joey was removed from an LD class in fifth grade, he sat in the back of the regular classroom crying softly. When his teacher asked what was wrong, Joey replied that he had never heard of the word the teacher was using. The instruction was over Joey's head, and he felt alone and betrayed. What was the word Joey had never heard? Colonies. The teacher was talking about the original thirteen colonies, and Joey, who had been in special classes for most of his school years, had never been introduced to social studies. His special education teacher had operated a self-contained class for students from first to sixth grades. She had to instruct in all subject areas in all grade levels for seventeen children. Reading instruction alone took two and one-half hours. After finishing math, spelling, handwriting, and language arts, the day was done. When was she to teach social studies and science to six different levels of students? She didn't have time, and Joey had, at eleven years of age and in the fifth grade, never heard of the original thirteen colonies.

Special education had promised to provide Joey with individualized instruction. How could any teacher not in a one-to-one situation possibly provide individual instruction to every one of seventeen children from six grade levels at the same time? The answer is that she could not, and Joey sat in the fifth grade classroom crying.

THESE ARE TRYING TIMES

Nearly every day in hundreds of schools, children are being put on trial. Multidisciplinary teams (MDTs) meet to discuss children and their failures. The bureaucrats are the prosecution, the judge, and the jury. There is no defense. The procedures are somewhat formal and the decisions are always the same—the child is guilty. What is he guilty of? Of not learning what he has been taught. The absurdity of that notion is profound, but nearly always overlooked. The belief is that a child is taught whether or not he learns.

Teachers spend time covering material. That is the term almost universally used. If the child did not learn the covered material, then the child is at fault. The teacher did her job. Most of the others got it, so anyone who did not get it must be blamed.

That is not to say that the teachers involved in this vicious plot are intentionally doing wrong. They are, in fact, doing what they believe to be right—what they have been taught—but that does not make it any less sinister.

NOTES

1. Dunn, L. M. (1968). Special education for the mildly retarded: Is much of it justifiable? *Exceptional Child*, 35, p. 6.

2. Davis, W. E. (1989). The regular education initiative debate: Its promise and problems. *Exceptional Children*, 55(5), 440-446.

3. Stainbach, S., & Stainbach, W. (1984). A rationale for the merger of special and regular education. *Exceptional Children*, 51, 475-476.

4. Carlberg, C., & Kavale, K. (1980). The efficacy of special versus regular class placement for exceptional children: A meta-analysis. *The Journal of Special Education*, 14(3), 295-309.

5. Sabatino, D. A. (1971). An evaluation of resource rooms for children with LD. *Journal of Learning Disabilities*, 4(2), 27-35.

6. Kavale, K. A. (1988). The long-term consequences of learning disabilities. In Wang, M. C., Reynolds, M. C., & Walberg, H. J. (Eds.). *Handbook of special education: Research and practice Volume 2 mildly handicapped conditions*. New York: Pergamon.

7. Epps, S., & Tindal, G. (1987). The effectiveness of differential programming in serving students with mild handicaps: Placement option and instructional programming. In M. C. Wang, M. C. Reynolds, & H. J. Walberg (Eds.). *Handbook of special education: Research and practice vol. 1 learner characteristics and adaptive education.* New York: Pergamon, p. 243.

8. Ibid., p. 243.

9. Wang, M. C., & Baker, E. T. (1985-86). Mainstreaming programs: Designs features and effects. *Journal of Special Education,* 19, 503-525.

10. Affleck, J. Q., Madge, S., Adams, A., & Lowenbraun, S. (1988). Integrated classroom versus resource model: Academic viability and effectiveness. *Exceptional Children,* 54(4), 339-348.

11. Gartner, A. (1986). Disabling help: Special education at the crossroads. *Exceptional Children,* 53(1), 72-76.

10

Science or Scientism?

*Science is always wrong. It never solves
a problem without creating ten more.*
G. B. Shaw

Have you ever walked into a room in the middle of a conversation? You may keep quiet for a while listening to what is being said. Eventually you hear things that you understand, but do not respond because you wonder what was said before. You do not want to say something that has already been said. Perhaps the people are well beyond what you have to offer. You may never enter the conversation, or, eventually, as you become more familiar with what is said, you may start joining in.

Scientific investigation is much like a conversation. First one party puts forth an idea; it is considered, and a second thought is put forth. Ideas are offered back and forth. If all goes well, things are gradually refined until at least a semblance of truth is achieved. Entering scientific investigation once it has begun is just like entering a conversation that you walked in on. You are not sure what has been said before, so you wait a while until you react.

THE LD CONVERSATION

The investigation concerning LD is also a conversation. The conversation may have had various starting times, but the late 1880s would be an appropriate time to think of as the start of the conversation since that is when educators began talking about *word blindness*. The conversation has continued until the present with most people believing that LD is a true disability. Some have taken the opposite view—LD is a myth. As the preface to Thomas Armstrong's book, *In Their Own Way*, begins:

> Six years ago I quit my job as a learning disabilities
> specialist. I had to. I no longer believed in learning
> disabilities.... I...began to see how this notion of learning
> disabilities was handicapping all of our children by
> placing the blame for a child's learning failure on
> mysterious neurological deficiencies in the brain
> instead of on much needed reforms in our systems of
> education. [1]

The existence of the condition of LD has not been proven
in any way, yet we have legislation declaring it to be a handicap
and that affects the ongoing conversation. People assume it
exists simply because it was declared a handicap by the legislature based on lobbying by special interest groups. Making it
even more difficult to join in the conversation is the fact that
they are using a foreign language—educationese. That, in effect,
excludes laypeople altogether. The speakers would have you
believe that all is based on research and fact. Eventually someone sees through the conversation, like Armstrong. What usually
happens is that those people get discouraged and walk away.

ARE TENDENCIES SCIENCE?

What we say and think about children says a lot about
ourselves. Most of the research in the social sciences has to do
with the beliefs held by those doing the research. They believe
that they can uncover some undisclosed truth, some fact, or
notion that will alter our thinking and give insight. The professors of social science are addicted to abstractions and generaliza-
tions and seek to find them under every rock. Tendencies are the
stuff research is made of. Even when there are no statistically significant findings, they talk of the direction of the findings being
toward something. Each author publishes findings, seeking to be
revered, promoted, and quoted. They believe that with each piece
of scientific research, they are leading us closer to the truth,
whatever that is. Yet, with the volumes being written every year,
there is a sameness that is stultifying.

They say the same things over and over, and the answers
are all the same. They pretend that we now know something that
we did not know, and the information they give us will bring us
closer to the truth—the ultimate generalization. Little time is
spent questioning the research or even reading it. The people
most likely to read research are other researchers or students

seeking to get something else published. Seldom do practitioners spend time reading research. When they do take the time, people file it under "Oh, that is interesting," or under "That guy doesn't know what he is talking about," and seldom use it to change how they approach instruction.

NUMBERS HIDE INEXACTNESS

Scientism prefers numbers to words and thought. Somehow attaching a number to something seems to make it more exact. A 3.0 grade reading level, an IQ of 116, a visual-motor age of 5 years 6 months—each sounds exact, complete, definitive. Figures are safe. How could anyone argue with a number? Once numbers are involved, it is no longer a subjective impression. Decisions based on those numbers become perfunctory. LD decisions, for example, become number decisions and seem like they are based on logic and fairness. If a student's scores on a battery of tests qualify the student for LD, it is the numbers that have done it. Numbers make educators appear aloof, free from prejudice.

LD is nearly universally accepted, just as witchcraft was accepted in the 1600s. Witches were found everywhere, and just because people were able to convince the masses that they existed, they really did. So it is with LD. If I can find any symptom occurring in more than one person, I can develop some syndrome to label those symptoms as disease. Because I sound authoritative, I can band together with my cohorts and convince the unassuming that implication equals fact. If I can somehow quantify a behavior, much the better. With such reasoning, science can now call a certain amount of alcohol consumption a disease; so, too, with gambling, child abuse, and even not reading.

IT DEPENDS

Just like every other human characteristic, social science has one universal truth—"It depends." is the answer to nearly any question. We cannot predict anything in the social sciences with certainty. That is particularly true in special education where Down syndrome children write books and star in television series. The professors who so strongly promote research are seeking to be recognized, to pretend to shed light on problems. They see the mishmash of research as somehow enlightening the

enlightened further while keeping all others in the dark. No one
can speak on a topic such as LD, unless one has read all that is
written and quoted the right authors.

The problem is that they develop their own specialized
jargon which gives the appearance of knowing something which
is simply not known. It also serves to increase the feelings of
importance while excluding the layperson. The educationists
talk in big words while saying very little. The facts they produce
seem to call for major pronouncements. Using words such as
diagnostician, prioritize, utilize, input, and *collaborative* makes
the user seem knowledgeable while saying little. The facts they
produce only seem to move us closer to truth.

FACTS

There is no lack of information in the LD field. There are
facts upon facts. Ask me a question and I can find something
about it. Has anyone studied IEP conferences? Yes. Team decisionmaking? Yes. Visual perception? Yes. The effects of fluor-
escent lighting on reading? Yes. How room colors affect learning? If sugared snacks affect achievement? Teacher's tone of
voice? Yes to those and thousands more. There are thousands of
graduate students writing thousands of dissertations. There are
journals for every subspecialty conceivable. It would be difficult
to name a topic that has not been studied. Yet, what do all of the
facts add up to? Whatever you want them to.

To some, the irreconcilable conclusion is that something
is wrong with a large population of school children—perhaps 25
percent or more—that need to be labeled as LD. Others look at the
same data and conclude that LD is a myth. Some believe that
many children can learn only in specially controlled
environments in which they monitor their sugar intake, provide
full spectrum lighting, keep them in groups of eight or fewer, and
allow them to curl up on the floor whenever they wish. Others
believe that good old-fashioned "readin', writin', and 'rithmetic,
taught to the tune of a hickory stick" is all that is needed.

TYPICAL RESEARCH

A look at what is happening in educational research helps
underscore my point. While I was writing this chapter, a copy of
the *Journal of School Psychology* arrived in the mail. One of the

articles dealt with the classification of students within the "special education nomenclature."[2] The conclusions were not startling or even surprising. The decision as to what to classify a student (especially as LD) has more to do with the referral question than with the results of the tests administered. The reasons for referrals to a psychologist for evaluation help determine if the student is found to be exceptional. The classification serves more to confirm the referral question than to shed light on the subject. Agreement with correct placements occurred about 67 percent or two-thirds of the time. That still means that one third of the time the psychologists were incorrect, a highly significant number if your child or my child were one of the 33 percent misdiagnosed. Much of the inaccuracy in the diagnosis came from labeling students who were not exceptional as being LD resulting in what may be considered false positives—labeling students as LD when they are in fact not LD.

Not only was the referral question a cause of misdiagnosis, apparently so were years on the job. The longer someone was employed as a school psychologist, the more likely the diagnosis of LD. Social factors such as expectations of employers, principals, and teachers were cited as possible reasons. The conclusions one could reach are innumerable, not the least of which is to fire every psychologist before he or she gets tenure. The study, while mildly interesting is not the stuff by which major advances are made. Who among us did not know that the way a question is framed may influence its outcome? Did we really need a study to point that out to us? Will anyone behave differently because of the study? No.

This study points out possible problems in the actual assignment of students but like most educational research, it is little more than the statement of the obvious in an obscure manner. Unfortunately, that seems to be a requirement of the conferring of degrees. If you want a Ph.D., then you had better write obscurely about the obvious.

MORE TYPICAL RESEARCH

A particularly germane example of writing obscurely about the obvious begins on page 81 of the same summer 1991 issue of the *Journal of School Psychology*. This study is typical of what is passed off as educational research. This study is the completion of the dissertation requirements of the first author and involves the playing of twenty questions. But since playing twenty questions is not scientific enough, the participants in the study "solved twenty questions tasks." How one solves a task I am not sure, but that is what the students were asked to do. Each task included a "visual array of 15 noun pictures." What is a visual array? What is a noun picture? Your guesses are as good as mine. The entire procedure seemed to be staged antics designed to get at some tremendously important and unanswered questions. Yet, the conclusions are so obvious that anyone who has half a brain already knew them. Let me state the authors' conclusions from the abstract:

> The results indicated that modeling procedures were effective in helping children in both age groups learn how to use constraint-seeking interrogative strategies, although better results were produced by cognitive than by exemplary modeling procedures. Regardless of the type of modeling that was provided, the older children learned this complex cognitive behavior more thoroughly than their younger counterparts.[3]

Those big words seem to convey a lot of important information, but what do they really mean? The conclusions are twofold. First, children learn to ask better questions if they are told how rather than just shown how; and, second, the older children did better than the younger children. Do we really need research to tell us those things?

That is not all, however. Just so teachers don't get too carried away in their rush to use this important information, the authors caution about generalizing the laboratory findings to actual classroom situations. Regardless, they tell readers that telling someone what to do is probably better than just showing. Of course, they tell readers in far bigger words. They don't recommend telling they recommend "providing detailed cognitive explanations." Again, I am not sure what the difference is between a cognitive explanation and a plain old explanation, but they really go out on a limb when they suggest that reading and mathematics might be curricular domains in which these strategies could be tried—cautiously I am sure. I wonder about social studies and science domains. Perhaps more research will be needed before we dare to "tell" students what to do in those areas.

Now it is fun to pick at such research, particularly because it is so easy to do. I am certain that someone could look at my dissertation and conclude that it also was useless, and I would probably agree. It was an exercise to get to the degree. But when such stuff is printed in journals, and such journals are used to prove that things are the way they are, we must begin to question if this is doing any good, and are we using this whole system to hurt children. I am sure little harm will come to children if teachers start "providing detailed cognitive explanations of skills being modeled." If fact, I am sure that more harm will come if they are not provided detailed cognitive explanations but save us from this trivial pursuit.

EDUCATIONESE

Just as the early bird gets the worm, the academician who uses big words gets the grant, gets published, and gets promoted. The use of big words gives even simple ideas the appearance of great assertions. Often it is merely the statement of the obvious such as "providing detailed cognitive explanations of skills being modeled." No one would publish statements of the obvious unless the obvious is obscured. In *The Graves of Academe*, Richard Mitchell wrestles with the language of educationism. He quotes the following passage:

> These instructional approaches are perhaps best conceived on a systems model, where instructional variables (input factors) are mediated by factors of students' existing cognitive structure (organizational properties of the learner's immediately relevant concepts in the particular subject field); and by personal predispositions and tolerance toward the requirements of inference, abstraction, and impulse control, all prerequisites to achievement in the discovery or the hypothetical learning mode.[4]

Mitchell concludes that this passage may mean, "that what a student learns depends on what he already knows and on whether or not he gives a damn." He goes on to say that, "if [the author] said it in plain English he wouldn't be allow to teach any course in it. Indeed, if he *could* say it in plain English, he would probably have enough good sense not to say it, thus disclosing to the world that years of study have brought him at last to a firm grasp of the obvious."[5]

A look at the field of learning disabilities shows many of the traits that Mitchell bemoans. Too often simple ideas are obscured. If they were said in plain English, they would never be said. Many researchers would argue that their language is complicated because the ideas are complicated. No doubt some of the ideas are complicated, but calling thinking a basic psychological process does not make it any more precise, it only makes it more obscure. The article I previously mentioned about the classification of students is entitled, "Classification Congruence among School Psychologists and Its Relationship to Type of Referral Question and Professional Experience."[6] What do you suppose congruence is? Do you think it means agreement? If so, why didn't the authors use the word *agreement* instead of choosing a word from mathematics which seems to imply something more than agreement? The answer is they chose it for that very reason—because it seems to imply something more than agreement but doesn't mean anything more than agreement. The language of scientism is to obscure rather than enlighten.

Even Ann Landers is consulted regarding the language of education. The following letter was included in her August 21, 1992 column:

> Dear Ann Landers: You are supposed to be a smart cookie. Can you figure this out? I bet my wife $10 you'd flunk just as we did.
>
> The parent of a Houston high school pupil received a message from the school principal concerning a special meeting on a proposed new educational program.
>
> The message read: " Our school's cross-graded, multiethnic, individualized learning program is designed to enhance the concept of an open-ended learning program with emphasis on a continuum of multiethnic, academically enriched learning, using the identified intellectually gifted child as the agent or director of his own learning. Major emphasis is on cross-graded, multiethnic learning with the main objective being to learn respect for the uniqueness of a person."
>
> The parent responded: "Dear Principal: I have a college degree, speak two foreign languages and know four Indian dialects. I've attended a number of county fairs and three goat ropings, but I haven't the faintest idea as to what the hell you are talking about." OK, Ann,

do YOU know what the principal was trying to say?—Two Dummies in Fort Worth

Dear Friends: I don't think you are dummies. That principal needs to learn how to express himself in simple terms.

What he means is: "We are planning a program for students of all races, which we hope will encourage the brighter ones to move ahead at their own speed. Grading will be geared to the learning level of the student. In this way, we hope to teach and grade each student according to his ability to learn." P.S. Pay your wife $10.

I am not so sure I would be willing to pay the $10. Multiethnic does not mean race—the Mexican-American children that make up a goodly portion of Houston's students are white. Second, the principal says the program is to "enhance the concept of an open-ended learning program" whatever that means; that "Major emphasis is on cross-graded, multiethnic learning"; and that "the main objective being to learn respect for the uniqueness of a person." None of that even mentions subject matter or moving ahead, much less moving ahead at one's own pace. I think the principal is describing a program to teach children about other cultures, beyond that I have no clue. What do you think? Educational jargon is used to confuse.

HYPOTHETICAL CONSTRUCTS

Most scientific terms are called hypothetical constructs. Constructions used to put forth a hypothesis. We can only define LD in the loosest of terms since it is merely a hypothesis manufactured out of someone's hunches and perceptions. Unfortunately, parents and educators begin treating the constructs as if they are real rather than merely peoples' views of the world.

A distinguishing feature of constructs is that they have multiple referents. That is also true of LD. For example, all definitions of LD assume average mental ability, but how is mental ability established? With the use of another construct—intelligence. Intelligence, or the converse, retardation, does not have one referent or dimension but can be viewed from several different points of view.

What exactly is intelligence? No one knows for sure. One may find many definitions of intelligence including Boring's circular definition: "measurable intelligence is simply what the tests of intelligence test."[7] Some have viewed intelligence as being a singular general factor or *g* factor.[8] Others have suggested that it is a composite of different abilities.[9] Depending on what you want to accomplish, you many change your definition.

MEASURING IQ

How does one measure intelligence? Intelligence tests sample a person's behavior and provide a score based on a comparison of performance to other people usually of the same age. There are as many different assessments as definitions.   The Stanford-Binet Intelligence Scale asks questions such as, What is the difference between a bird and a dog?[10] It also asks students to define words orally, to trace mazes, and to stack blocks.   The Peabody Picture Vocabulary Test asks a person to point to one of four pictures in response to a word read aloud.   The Arthur Adaptation of the Leiter has no oral directions.   Students are required to match blocks to pictures that are usually designs or concepts. The Goodenough-Harris Test scores the number of body parts included in a human figure drawn on a blank piece of paper.

Each of those tests provides a single score called an intelligence quotient, yet each looks at far different behaviors. There is no actual measurement of intelligence; rather achievement is measured and intelligence inferred.   One need only look at the asking of vocabulary questions common to many IQ tests to see the truth of that assertion.

NAMING WHAT WE SEE

Constructs never appear in nature in such a way that they can be readily observed. The researcher must define the category and specify the observable behaviors that must be present. This is called operationalizing the definition.   The major problem with this type of research is that people begin to assign to the construct a reality which is not there. There is no such thing as intelligence. It is merely an inference from a standardized set of questions or behaviors.

This nominalization becomes very difficult to deal with because the nature of our language is to treat nouns as if they are real. This is particularly true in the case of LD where we start talking about children having LD rather than recognizing it as a hypothetical construct used to help us deal with groups of children with similar behaviors. It has been asserted that:

> Like all other labels in use in the realm of psychological disorders, [LD] is only a description and not an explanation of the problem one has observed. If a child has trouble learning and someone labels him or her learning-disabled, there is always the danger that, having found an impressive-sounding label for the child, efforts at providing help will cease because the label is viewed as an explanation for the problem. The statement "He has a learning disability, so of course he can't be expected to learn" all too often serves as an excuse for giving up on efforts to teach such a child. When used in this manner, the term "learning disability" is clearly objectionable.[11]

Furthermore, the question of one having LD is raised with the following:

> Is one justified in saying that he "has" a learning disability? The best one can ever do is to say that a child fails to reflect learning through changes in performance under the ordinary teaching methods which have been tried so far.[12]

Unfortunately, nouns used to label abstractions control our thinking and lead us into thinking that they are real.

THE MYTH OF LEARNING DISABILITIES

LD speculation is helpful in allowing us to look at learning in different ways, but somehow what is mere speculation has become truth by virtue of its adoption into federal law. That is especially disturbing when there has never been agreement about LD. In fact, some have flatly stated that there is no such thing as LD. Thomas McKnight states:

> In theory, the use of the term "learning disability" provides a point of reference for communicating about youngsters who are having difficulty in school for no apparent psychological, medical, or social reason. "By emphasizing that these children have trouble learning, the term places the responsibility for helping such

children squarely in the realm of education".... However, "it should by now be clear that *there is no such thing as learning disability* [italics added]... [that it is] not an immutable entity that somehow exists in its own right" (pp. 6-7). Too often, in fact, this relatively impressive label for the child denotes the end of assistance. The label is viewed as the explanation for the learning difficulty, and the educational system is given a mythical scapegoat for its failure to educate a segment of the school population. [13]

The problem with the science surrounding LD and much of the rest of social science is that with its specialized jargon, the layperson is excluded from the investigation. The average person can only listen to the conversation and get a dim view of what is going on. The implication is that whatever occurred in the past is incorrect and flawed, new methods will be found that are correct and helpful. We are taught to forgo common sense. Research will discover the truth. Unfortunately, the child who is not learning has become the scapegoat for education's failure.

NOTES

1. Armstrong, T. (1987). *In their own way: Discovering and encouraging your child's personal learning style.* New York: St. Martin's Press, p. ix.

2. Ward, S. B., Ward, T. J., Jr., & Clark III, H. T. (1991). Classification congruence among school psychologists and its relationship to type of referral question and professional experience. *Journal of School Psychology.* 29,89-108.

3. John, K. M., Gutkin, T. B., & Plake, B. S. (1991). Use of modeling to enhance children's interrogative strategies. *Journal of School Psychology.* 29, 81-88.

4. Mitchell, R. (1981). *The graves of academe.* Boston: Little, Brown, p. 33.

5. Ibid., p. 33.

6. Ward, Ward, & Clark III. Classification congruence.

7. Boring, E. G. (1923). Intelligence as the tests test it. *New Republic,* 6, 35-37.

8. Spearman, C. (1904). General intelligence objectively measured and determined. *American Journal of Psychology,* 15, 201-293.

9. Guilford, J. P. (1959). *Personality.* New York: McGraw-Hill.

10. Terman, L. M., & Merrill, M.A. (1960). *Stanford-Binet intelligence scale.* Boston: Houghton Mifflin.

11. Ross, A. O. (1976). *Psychological aspects of learning disabilities & reading disorders*. New York: McGraw-Hill, p. 2-3.

12. Ibid., p. 6.

13. McKnight, R. T. (1982). The learning disability myth in American education. *Journal of Education, 164*(4), 351-359.

11

Increasing Children's Options

The average learner is a myth.
Peter Kline

Picture a rainbow, then, imagine the color blue becoming gradually more and more powerful until all you can see is blue. The blue takes over so slowly and in such a way that you are not aware of the subtle shift. Seeing only the color blue in such a way is like a mind-set. As long as you assume that blue is all there is, you are stuck in your mind-set. It is just like the Indian tribe that has only three words to describe the colors of the spectrum. They see red, orange, and yellow as one color. They have no other options. They are stuck in a world of three colors. They do not see red and yellow as distinct from orange and never will unless they become unstuck. In much the same way, we have become stuck in our mind-set about LD. The assumptions, beliefs, and expectations that we have about LD children control our thinking. We have other options we could consider about LD children, but they are options that we don't see because of our mind-set. A mind-set is really a belief system.

BELIEF SYSTEMS

In his book on handling discipline problems in school, Michael Valentine discusses what he refers to as erroneous belief systems which people use to explain away student misbehavior.[1] Holidays, teacher demands, hyperactivity, childhood stages, socioeconomic status, brain damage, and emotional deprivation are some reasons teachers give for student misbehavior. Valentine cites teachers in Los Angeles who say, "If it rains for more than two days, we can't possibly control the students because of all that pent-up energy. They get real 'squirrely'."[2] In more than two days, we can't possibly control the students because of all that pent-up energy. They get real 'squirrely'."[2] In the belief system of those teachers, two days of rain causes children to misbehave. Valentine wonders how teachers in Oregon, where it rains for weeks at a time. ever control children. Other teachers in the Los Angeles area, for example, believe students are uncontrollable when the winds blow in from the desert. Some people believe that being a first child, an only child, a middle child, the only boy in a family of girls, the only girl in a family of boys, being raised by a single parent, being raised by older parents, and other such things cause misbehavior.

The problems with those explanations, and the others listed by Valentine, is that the people who cite those reasons never view children as being capable and responsible. Instead, they see children as victims of circumstances and unable to rise above those circumstances. Only when adults see children as capable and responsible regardless of circumstances will the adults act in ways to make the children do what is required whether it is sitting in a seat or learning to read. Otherwise, adults will lower expectations and provide excuses. LD is just one of the many excuses used to view children as being victims, as being incapable and not responsible. If asked, most teachers would tell you that LD is an explanation of why Johnny or Janey cannot read when, in fact, it is only a statement that Johnny or Janey is not reading.

That is true of many medical diagnoses as well. Dermatitis, conjunctivitis, and many of the other itises that affect humans are really only Latin terms describing what is already known. If you have a rash, a doctor will tell you that you have dermatitis and prescribe some cream that you probably could get without a prescription. *Derma* refers to skin, and *itis* means inflammation. Thus, *dermatitis* means inflammation of the skin, nothing more. The doctor really has only parroted your symptoms back to you in Latin terms, but you think you have an explanation for the rash on your arm.

If your eyes are red and swollen, chances are that you have conjunctivitis. Many a medical doctor will diagnose and treat you for that. But what is conjunctivitis? The dictionary tells you it is "inflammation of the conjunctiva." Conjunctiva being "the mucous membrane that lines the inner surface of the eyelids and is continued over the forepart of the eyeball." So what do you know about your eye problem when you learn that you have conjunctivitis? You learn that you have an inflammation of the area around the eye. You know nothing more than you did, except that you have a medical term for it.

Such is the case with most of the labels of education as well. We do not know what LD is, except that it is whatever the powers that be decide that it is. It sounds like it is something more than a statement about being an underachiever but that is all LD really means. The only question is how low must someone be achieving to be called LD. In 1975 when PL 94-142 was passed, only 2 percent of the population could have LD, whatever it was. Now, any number can. In different states, there are different requirements and different levels of identification. In effect, PL 94-142 provided legislatively approved segregation for underachievers.

EARLY EXPERIENCES

What you see is what you get. That phrase, made popular on the old TV show "Laugh In," has frequently been interpreted to mean more than what it first appears to mean. It also has been used to suggest that your mind-set, what you see, determines what you get. If you are of a mind to see things a certain way, that is how they appear to you. Doctors in Moliere's day saw bleeding patients as a cure for many illnesses; thus when someone came to them with a certain illness, they used bleeding as a technique. Nowadays, doctors dispense drugs for nearly any problem—from difficulty sitting still to drug addiction. Twentieth-century doctors view nearly every human problem from a medical point of view and act accordingly. They often overlook the most important component in behavior—early experiences.

Elephants are perhaps the most powerful animals in the world. They can uproot trees with their enormous strength, yet many of us have seen huge elephants with ropes around their legs tied to wooden stakes driven into the ground. The elephants stand passively never attempting to free themselves from such a minor restraint. Why? Why don't they simply pull up the stakes and free themselves? The answer has to do with early training. When elephants are born and their strength has not developed, they are chained to steel stakes embedded in concrete. The small elephants tug and tug at the chains, but to no avail. Eventually, they come to accept the fact that they cannot get away, and they give up trying. From that point on, they never again try to escape.

The baby elephants have learned that whenever something is tied around their legs, they cannot get away. The learning is complete and permanent. For the rest of their lives, a rope and a wooden stake is all that is needed as a reminder that they are unable to move. Their early experiences have defined their behavior and limited their options.

CHILDREN'S EARLY EXPERIENCES

So it is with LD children. Not all children come to school with the same skills, abilities, and knowledge. Although we, as people, often celebrate our differences, school is not one of the places where we do. Differences are seen as deviance. For example, while some children can learn the alphabet easily in kindergarten, others do not. There may be many reasons why they do not learn the alphabet and all sorts of other things—some having to do with ability, interest, motivation, fear, lack of experiences, and the like. But the fact remains that most children learn the alphabet in kindergarten; some do not and they are seen as being deviant, at-risk, or second class. Those children may not learn the alphabet in kindergarten, but they learn something just as lasting. They learn that they are inferior. Like the baby elephants learn to limit themselves, so do the children who did not master the alphabet. When they eventually become capable of learning the alphabet and all of the other stuff, they may not learn it just as the elephants do not try to uproot the stake because, at an early age, those children learned that they cannot learn and have given up. Their experiences have limited their options.

THE FIRST DAY OF SCHOOL

Imagine the first day of school for the average child. Those of you who are parents can remember your child getting on the school bus for the first day of kindergarten and all the accompanying feelings—the pride, the sense of loss, the happiness, and the fear. Your children faced many of those same feelings but from a five year old's perspective. There was no more mom or dad or big brother or sister or grandma or anyone else to help them out. They must get on the bus, find a seat, get off the bus, walk through the hallway, greet the teacher, take off their coats, hang them up, find their seats, meet new friends, and follow all sorts of new directions by themselves. "Line up." "Raise your hand to go to the bathroom." "Do not speak if someone else is speaking." "Sit up with both feet on the floor." "Keep you hands to yourself." The list is endless, and the many new elements facing them are nearly overwhelming. For some, they are over-whelming.

Most of the procedures in school are not designed in the best interests of the children but are for the smooth running of the schools. There is plenty of room for fear and failure and second-guessing from little five year olds. Those first experiences are often decisive in forming a child's view of himself as part of school and overall society. If he doesn't know the difference between b and d and everyone else does, he may form a view of himself that does not allow him to learn it later. He may become stuck in his poor self-image. A rope and a wooden stake may hold him down the rest of his life.

It only stands to reason that the younger and less secure children are when they experience negative feedback, the more apt it is to affect them for the remainder of their school years and beyond. Emotions are powerful and will influence all that they do. Schools can be sterile, scary places that force many powerful emotions to surface. Those emotions produce images and beliefs of how children see themselves. Just like seeing everything blue, thoughts such as, "I'm not good at math," or "I'll never learn to read," or "I am a Little Dummy (LD)" will create mind-sets, that may never be eliminated.

SCHOOL EXPERIENCES

Students make assumptions about themselves and about school having to do with how they think adults want them to perform. Schools and teachers can be coercive, threatening, and punishing. They can rob students of freedom. Students are told when to get up, when to sit, if they can have a snack, or talk to a friend. Even if they are truly troubled by something, the teacher may say, "Not now. Can't you see I'm busy."

Beyond that, children are quizzed and put on display. They are ridiculed and poked fun of. Think back to when you were in school. Did you enjoy all of your teachers? Were there any who intimidated you, made you feel stupid, called you names, or asked you to recite when it was clear you did not know an answer? Did you ever have to write a problem on the board when you did not know how to do it? Were any of your classmates subjected to such fate?

Even if most teachers are kind and loving most of the time, a particularly emotional incident can overshadow all other experiences. I spoke to a girl who was a senior in high school whose most vivid memory of school was being called four-eyes by a teacher in elementary school. The teacher may have thought he was being funny or affectionate, but in fact, he was inflicting psychological pain.

Another student told me how she felt when she baked a cake for a birthday party and the teacher refused a piece because it was not made from scratch. Another student was told in math class that he belonged "down the hall in with the other dummies." How deeply can teachers' comments affect a person's life? I sold a car to a woman who introduced herself to me as Bird. She was in her thirties and had a teenage daughter. I asked her if Bird was her given name. She told me that when she was in school a teacher called her "bird brain" and the name had stuck. The name had stuck so completely that twenty years later, when she introduced herself to a stranger she was calling herself Bird. What a tremendously negative impact that teacher had on her.

THE FEELINGS OF A YOUNGSTER

Not all teachers call students names, most are compassionate and caring, but circumstances may also have a profound effect. Imagine the emotionally immature five or six year old being exposed to the feelings that accompany not knowing something. Then imagine the teacher accentuating those feelings by asking the child to read aloud or put the problem on the board. Even if the teacher were open and supportive, it still hurts not to know something, especially if you think everyone else knows it. Even if the teacher were completely supportive, the child will have come to the situation with many feelings from other teachers or other days with the same teacher. Remember ducking down behind the kid in front of you, trying to sit still to avoid calling attention to yourself? Did you ever forget to do your homework? Was it easy to tell the teacher? There was lots of pain associated with those feelings, wasn't there?

In school, kids learn to anticipate what the teachers want and try to perform to their expectations. When a teacher calls on a student who does not know an answer, if the teacher is impatient, the student learns that if he says nothing, the teacher quickly calls on someone else. Soon those students learn that not answering is an easy way to get the teacher off their backs. In fact, research has shown that teachers are more patient with smart children than with children they do not believe will know an answer.

Children learn many such coping mechanisms. Of the sixty low-achieving students who were the subject of Karen Zelan's book, *The Risks of Knowing*, thirty-seven "seemed to blanket their minds with feigned boredom and stupidity." Some even faked the personality of the mentally retarded.[3] The children, according to Zelan, were afraid of learning and used those ruses to keep from learning. Teachers and parents may unwittingly become participants in those charades by looking for what children do wrong. Adults spend too much time catching children being bad. How much better would it be to catch the child being good to offer opportunities in which they will succeed? I remember when I was in seventh grade, one of my classmates, who was very bright, began asking a series of stupid questions. Edgar asked one stupid question after the other, each of them seemingly pointless and out of character. When I began to laugh, the teacher admonished me and proceeded to answer each question. Later, Edgar told me that he did not have his homework completed, and he had discovered that if he asked some dumb questions, the teacher wouldn't call on him anymore. The teacher fell for the trick.

THE CAUSES OF STUPIDITY

Sometimes teachers cause the stupidity. Self-images are mind-sets based on previous experiences. Labeling a child as LD involves lumping together similar behaviors and giving them a title. This lumping has a power of its own. The phenomenon works all of the time when we put labels on children. When we say lazy, we are saying more about ourselves than about the other person. A teacher who says a student is lazy has told me about how little he has done to provide interesting and motivating school work. This teacher does not believe in the child. There is no such thing as a child who is lazy. There are only children who need to feel free to try different things. Despite what the popular notions suggest, reading is an easy skill to learn. Nearly everyone learns to read. The few who don't learn as quickly as the other children are labeled as being in some way deficient. The label depends upon the person doing the labeling, but it confirms the students' lack of achievement and gives them an excuse for it. Children who do not learn to read as quickly as their peers, are labeled and put into remedial programs, reinforcing their underachievement. Calling students deficient and removing them from regular reading instruction can only lead to further learning delays.

CAN'T-ING

Have you ever felt like you could not do something? Whether it is building a house, making a dress, or changing the spark plugs, most of us have developed some can'ts. Because we are unwilling to allow ourselves to fail, we resort to can't-ing: I can't build a house. I can't make a dress. I can't swim. I can't. I can't. I can't. We convince ourselves of our can'ts.

The never-ending parade of tests in school shows what students can't do. If Johnny gets a low score in a mathematics standardized test, it means he can't do math. If he scores low in reading, he can't read. Let's steer him away from math and reading and into something he can do. If a student does not score well in academic achievement tests, it is assumed that he will be good at working with his hands. How about sending him to the vo-tech?

We could assume different things, such as *if someone scores low on math, it could mean he is a prime candidate to learn math.* Teachers should view low scorers as challenges rather than defeats. If I were a golf instructor, I think I could teach more to a beginner than to an advanced student and the improvement would be greater. I would see a beginner as providing me with more opportunity to teach. The same should be said of the poor reader. He is ripe to learn. Instead we convince ourselves that the raw material is deficient, and we do not try.

LEARNED HELPLESSNESS

A study that helped Martin Seligman develop his theory about learned helplessness involved providing a mild electrical shock to dogs who were in small boxes. The dogs were given a shock while a tone was sounded. It was hypothesized that the dogs would soon associate the tone with being shocked and would react to the tone as if it were a shock. Once the association was established, the dogs were put into boxes with a board across the middle. Then a shock was administered. The idea was that the dogs would jump over the barrier and escape the shock. Later, instead of a shock, the tone would be substituted to see if the dogs attempted to avoid the tone by jumping over the barrier.

There was a fundamental problem with the research. When placed in the second box, the dogs never tried to get away from the shock. Apparently, the dogs had accidentally learned a tremendous lesson; they had learned that they were helpless in avoiding shocks. In the first box, they had no escape route since that was not the intent of that part of the experiment. Unfortunately, they never tried to get away from the shocks in other circumstances when they easily could have. When an escape route was introduced, the dogs did not seek to escape, they stayed and took the shocks. They had previously learned that it was impossible to get away from the shocks. Their learning was so complete that they no longer tried to escape under any circumstance. Just like the baby elephants, they had learned to stop trying. They had learned to be helpless.

LD IS LEARNED HELPLESSNESS

I honestly believe that very, very few of the students we label as LD and who grow up to be adults who can't read are really helpless. Reading is a skill that can be taught like any other skill. Given the right circumstances, people learn once they have overcome the can'ts that have been built up during their formative years. The human brain is so efficient that it is always learning. Unfortunately, some of the learning involves becoming helpless just like Seligman's dogs. Children may not be ready for the direct instruction provided in schools and, instead, learn something else—such as "I am dumb or lazy or disabled."

Albert Einstein was not a good student. He did not speak until he was three and one-half and did not speak well until he was ten, yet he is considered by most to be the foremost thinker of the twentieth century. One can only guess what would have happened if Einstein would have been given a preschool screening test at three years of age and had been declared at-risk or language delayed. He would have been placed in a special or remedial program and after a few weeks of learning that he was defective, he probably would have agreed and quit trying.

LEARNING NOT TO ACHIEVE

As long as educators see learning problems as existing within the child little will be done to change. Why should anything be done? Most children, even those placed with the worst teachers, learn to read, don't they? It must not be the fault of the curriculum or the teachers. There must be something wrong with the child who doesn't learn at the same time his peers learn. The children who do not learn as quickly as the others are eventually labeled and segregated.

Underachievement, learning disabilities, reading disabilities, dyslexia, and all the rest of the labels are such a hodgepodge that it is difficult to separate into groups what is being talking about. Even if someone were to define what he is talking about, the next person will contradict and argue for a different definition. There is no consensus regarding LD definitions, but the fact remains that a large number of un-derachieving youngsters have great difficulty with reading. The more severe are called dyslexic or learning disabled. I believe that nearly all of the children are the result of inappropriate instruction and inappropriate curriculum.

There is no unanimity among LD experts. There are many who have spoken out against LD. The critics of special education have concluded that real LD exists in very few cases. It is worth repeating what I cited in chapter 2, Mary Burkhardt said, "The child who is truly reading disabled (dyslexic) is *very rare* [italics added]."[4] Gerald Coles concluded that "After decades of research, it has still not been demonstrated that disabling neurological dysfunctions exist in more than a *minuscule number* of these children [italics added]."[5] Even proponents of LD recognize that many of the children labeled as LD are created by life experiences. Hilde Mosse has written one of the most complete books on lear-ning disabilities. In it, she uses the terms *psychogenic* and *socio-genic* reading disorders to refer to students for whom no organic basis can be found for learning disorders.[6] Apparently the ex-planation for reading failure in those cases has to do with life experiences, hardly a clear-cut case for damaged brains.

James Ysseldyke and his colleagues at Minnesota found that 75 percent of regular education students who were not labeled as LD could be labeled as LD. They also found that there was no way of distinguishing the so-called LD students from garden-variety underachievers. The conclusion was reached that the definitions of LD are broad enough to include the majority of normal children, so that *most children who are referred to be tested will be declared eligible for special education services.* After that, the decisions have little to do with the data collected since the data do not distinguish a separate groups of students.[7]

ALIBIS

Rudolf Flesch in *Why Johnny Still Can't Read* presented what he referred to as his ten favorite alibis for reading failure. He explained them briefly and then devoted a chapter to each alibi. All of the chapters are germane to the present discussion, but of particular interest is the chapter "Your Child Is Disabled." Flesch begins the chapter by quoting Dr. Dale Bryant from Teachers College, Columbia University, that LD is caused by the teaching methods used. Flesch quotes twelve other scholars from the reading field who are convinced that dyslexia (or LD), except in rare cases, is the result of instructional methods. Flesch gives examples of true dyslexics and of the far more common imitation LDers. His conclusion is that the term *learning disability* is:

> soothing as you can get if you have to tell a couple of worried parents that their child is sick...the definition is wide as a barn door and wholly negative.... The main thing is it is never the school's or the method's fault, but the fault of the poor victim.[8]

A BELIEF SYSTEM THAT WORKS

All children are lovable, capable, and responsible. Never have I met a young child who was truly mean or nasty. Some may act that way, but get them alone, away from their families and peers, and that facade disappears. From birth to entrance into school, nearly all parents believe their children are special. The parents marvel as the children grow and learn quickly what is often not even taught. By the time the child reaches school age, the parents and grandparents are captivated with the natural curiosity and creativity expressed by America's young, but then school starts, and some children who could not wait to start kindergarten begin hating school. They no longer come to school eager and willing. Instead, they express displeasure and talk of hating school. By twelfth grade even the most accomplished of students sees it for what it is, a dull wasteland of work sheets and short answer tests.

ONCE THE BELL RINGS

Students are alive with questions, fun, joy, and activity until the bell rings. Then they become zombies and go through the motions. The little ones circle the ducks, and the older ones write reports on books they never read (and probably the teacher has never read). The teachers drone on while the students pass notes and look out the windows. The students are not the only ones who become zombies. The teachers do, too. They get out their teacher's manuals and follow the steps. No thought goes into what they are doing. There doesn't need to be any. The publishers have taken the thought away.

There are exceptions. Some lessons are exciting. Some teachers have a gift for teaching. Some schools seem alive, and the children seem to enjoy themselves, but most of us have learned that school is not fun. It is drudgery. Children must be prepared for life; they must learn that life is not all fun and games.

We accept that kind of thinking as truth without ever questioning. We think we are supposed to be teaching children how to think and how to learn. We try to invent ways of making students think, but children already know how to think. They came to school thinking, and they think all the while they are there. Most schools give us none of the sense of thinking. I dare any of you parents who do not remember school to go spend a few days in school with your child. Sit in the back of the room and watch the children in the elementary grades filling out ditto sheets while the teacher is with her reading groups, or go to a high school Spanish class if you want real boredom. How about sitting through an English class while children diagram sentences or conjugate verbs?

WHAT TO DO

"If it works, keep doing it. If it doesn't work, stop doing it." This is a piece of advice I often give to parents and teachers. On the surface, no one would argue with that tenet. If you are not getting the results you want, change something, but sometimes the simplest of advice is the hardest to take. I have heard people

call children liars over and over again, or worse names in a effort
to change their behavior. The opposite usually happens. Call
someone a liar often enough and you produce a liar. Although I
am not sure at what point a person becomes a liar. After one lie?
After six lies? After lying every day for a week? If it is true that
when a person tells a lie, she becomes a liar, then if a liar tells the
truth does she become a truth-teller? If one lie can condemn a
person to the status of liar then one truth should also retrieve her
from that status. Correct?

But that is not how negative labels work. They become
ingrained and permanent. Fortunately, positive labels can work
the same way if properly applied. A good example of how positive
labels can work is provided by Esther Rothman in her book, *The
Angel Inside Went Sour*. Rothman writes:

> A girl caught sneaking out of the building without per-
> mission hurls at me, "If I left this building, then my
> mother is a whore, and my mother ain't no whore, and I
> never left this stinkin building."
>
> Or another girl, caught with cigarette in hand in
> the bathroom, may scream, "If I smoked in the bathroom,
> my mother is dead and my mother ain't dead, so you're
> a...liar, I didn't smoke in no bathroom."
>
> A girl refusing to follow instructions taunts, "If I
> do that, my mother is a faggot and my mother ain't a
> faggot so I'm not doing it."
>
> Should I blame them for being more creative
> than I, or should I somewhat envy them for their existing
> powers? I envy. I also fervently hope that I can give them
> some of my social judgment in exchange for some of their
> creativity. We have a lot to teach each other, and we do.
>
> "That's very creative," I respond. "You have an
> unusual way of saying things. You also have an unusual
> way of seeing them."
>
> Each girl gets the point, namely she and I both
> know that she has lied. We also know that her lie has not
> worked. A new and exciting idea, however, has hit
> her—the concept that she is creative, and while she has
> been creative in a way that has not served her purpose,
> she might try to utilize her talents in more socially
> acceptable ways.
>
> And she does begin to try. [9]

Most of us would call the girls liars and alienate them.
Rothman finds a way of letting them know that she knows

without costing them their egos. She gives them something positive—they are creative. Neurolinguistic programming refers to what Rothman did as reframing—looking at something in a different way. This reframing is used to help the girls see themselves differently. When Rothman told the girls that they had an unusual way of saying things, it was a compliment. It allowed the girls to know that they were wrong without hurting their already damaged egos. And it also gave them something to feel good about.

ALL CHILDREN ARE
LOVABLE AND CAPABLE

When children are viewed as lovable and capable, great things can happen. Most of you have heard of Marva Collins and her school in Chicago which she started in one of the bedrooms of her house. She took the children who were the most difficult to manage or teach and taught them to succeed. She expected seven and eight year olds to read Shakespeare and Greek tragedies. And she always complimented them. If a child came to school dirty, she would not scold him in typical fashion or treat him to a harangue about the benefits of cleanliness. Instead, she would reach right to the child's need to be loved, and would say, "You have such a beautiful face and hands. Why don't you wash them so I can see them better?" Education needs more Rothmans and Collinses.

Acceptance of the notion that all children are lovable and capable will change things for the better. When children are viewed in that way, regardless of their behavior or their supposed abilities the results teachers get will be great.

LEARNING TO BE HELPLESS IN SCHOOL

The typical kindergarten is a hodgepodge of students and abilities. We tend to think of five year olds as being the same, but there are great differences. One student may have just missed the cutoff for attending school last year and will turn six on the first day of school. Another child may have just made the cutoff for this school year and will turn five the day before school begins. Is it fair for a student who just turned five to compete with a child who lacks one day of being 20 percent older? Of course not. The older child has 20 percent more life experiences from which to draw as well as a more developed body and thinking system.

Add to the difference in ages the fact that boys seem to mature at a slower rate than girls, perhaps six months slower at this age. Thus, if the older student were a girl and the younger a boy, there might be eighteen months difference in developmental age in a child that is only sixty months to begin with. Now, suppose that the older child, a girl, comes from a family in which the parents are both college-educated and have read to her since birth. Imagine further that she is the oldest or else an only child.

Assume that the younger student, the boy, is the fourth of six children in which neither of the parents is college educated and both must work. The mother works evenings as a cashier at a grocery store. The kids are in bed by the time she gets home. The father does not read very well, or just plain has his hands full in coming home from work and taking care of six children while his wife works. So, no one ever reads to the children.

On the first day of school, or whenever the kindergarten teacher starts teaching about Mr. A, Mr. B, and all of the other letters, the girl is prepared. She knows the alphabet. She is mature for a kindergartner and is confident in adult company. The boy, on the other hand, is barely ready for school, has never heard of the alphabet (except that he learned some nonsense sounds to sing a song that pleased his mother and grandparents), and sees very few adults.

What do you suppose will happen on that fateful day the teacher inflates Mr. A and begins instruction about the alphabet? The girl will raise her hand confidently and answer all the questions. The boy will be confused. If, for the next 180 days, the girl knows the answers, and the boy is unsure time after time, he will have learned that he cannot compete. He will be thinking, "Uh-oh, I hope the teacher doesn't call on me." He will have learned, just like the baby elephant, that there is no use trying when it comes to letters or numbers, and he will stop trying. Virtually nothing we do in school will get him to stop thinking of himself as incapable. He will have learned to be an underachiever.

Once a label, such as underachiever, is applied, it becomes a self-fulfilling prophecy. There is no need for him to ever try to read in school. He has learned that reading is hard to do—that he cannot keep up with the others. Once he is labeled, his parents and teachers know that he is wired up wrong—that there is some subtle, predisposition toward not learning letters, even though he could drive the garden tractor at five, play Super Mario on his Nintendo, build platforms for his minibike to jump, and learn the lyrics to dozens of pop songs.

STOP BANGING YOUR HEAD AGAINST THE WALL

Another example of early events affecting later behavior involved an experiment with northern pike. Apparently pike love minnows so an experimenter devised a somewhat cruel experiment in which pike were put into one side of a glass a-quarium. The aquarium was divided by a glass wall. Minnows were put on the other side of the aquarium, and you can guess what happened. The pike started banging their heads into the glass partition trying to eat the minnows on the other side. The more they tried, the harder they banged their heads. Eventually they quit trying just as the baby elephants quit trying. They had learned that they could not eat the minnows.

Then the experimenters removed the glass partitions from the aquarium, and the minnows and pike intermingled. The pike never again tried to eat the minnows. They had banged their heads so often that they had learned that there was no use trying. The minnows could swim into the faces of the pike and not be eaten. The pike would die before they would bang their heads against the wall again.

A young boy in kindergarten may have banged his head against the wall in trying to learn the letters that seemed to come so easily to the other children. After a while, he quit trying and, like the pike, would rather starve than try to learn anything that he knew he could not learn. You see, every child in school learns. Some learn the curriculum that is taught, others learn to be helpless and to give up. Eventually, they learn to stop banging their heads against the wall.

NOTES

1. Valentine, M. R. (1987). *How to deal with discipline problems in the schools: A practical guide for educators*. Dubuque: Kendall/Hunt.

2. Ibid., p. 44.

3. Zelan, K. (1991). *The risks of knowing*. New York: Plenum.

4. Burkhardt, M. (1981). Introduction. In Flesch, R. *Why Johnny still can't read.* New York: Harper & Row, p. xx.

5. Coles, G. (1987). *The learning mystique.* New York: Pantheon, p. xii.

6. Mosse, H. L. (1982). *You can prevent or correct learning disorders; The complete handbook of children's reading disorders.* New York: Teachers College Press.

7. Ysseldyke, J. E., Algozzine, B., Shinn, M. R., & McGue, M. (1982). Similarities and differences between low achievers and students classified as learning disabled. *Journal of Special Education,* 16, 73-85.

8. Flesch, R. F. (1981). *Why Johnny still can't read.* New York: Harper, p 146.

9. Rothman, E. P. (1972). *The angel inside went sour.* New York: Bantam, p. 40.

12

Predestination

For fools rush in where angels fear to tread.
Pope

It was one of those discussions that you hate to lose. I am not sure how it got started, but I was sure how it ended. Another school psychologist and I were discussing LD. He was arguing for a biologically determined view of LD. He looked at things like hair whorls and handedness to determine if someone was at-risk for LD. I was arguing for LD being a learned condition, saying that children could learn to read regardless of their biology. My colleague made his final statement and blew me out of the water. He said, "Ultimately, all behavior is biological." In that statement he had said it all. At the time, I thought he was right. There was no more to be said. I had lost the argument. He left, and left me confused.

I started thinking, Well, he is right. All behavior can ultimately be reduced to some biological component. That's what the professor had argued for in that psychology class I had taken years ago—a theory that ran counter to the prevailing theory of the 1970s—behaviorism. At that time, Skinnerian behaviorism was seen as the explanation of all behavior, at least from a psychologist's point of view. The psychologists who favored behaviorism referred to themselves as radical behaviorists and were fanatical in their beliefs about behavior. Animals, and therefore people, only learn responses to stimuli.

Behaviorists referred to whatever occurred in the body between a stimulus and a response as intervening variables, a clever way to conceptualize thought. Whatever was occurring in the body was viewed as something to be noticed, but of little importance. Some of the radical behaviorists, perhaps because of their radical thinking, even viewed those variables as part of the response itself. They were part of the responses that the stimulus produced. Chemical and biological reactions in the brain were behaviors and were caused by the stimulus. There was no free will involved in behavior. It was all determined by previous programming. That was the opposite of the argument that my colleague had laid on me—a person's biology determines behavior. Behaviorists countered that argument by claiming that biological and chemical reactions were part of the behavior itself, and the behavior was determined by pervious stimulus-response programming.

PREDESTINATION

Interestingly, that theory was, to my way of thinking, no different from my colleague's biological argument. The conclusion on either side suggested that behavior is predestined—either by biology or previous experiences. People became LD because of defective biology or inappropriate responses to stimuli. Behaviorism believed that people became LD because of their programming. Believers in natural explanations saw LD being caused by faulty genes or neural transmitters. Two different views but really the same view because there was no choice involved.

The idea of predestination was put forth by the Presbyterians in the 1800s. The theory was that God was not limited in time as we are: since He can see the future, and since He knows whether you will make it to heaven, in effect, your future has been determined before you act. Your actions are not really yours, for if you act in concert with God's laws, you are merely acting out a part determined for you. There is no glory for you. Your behavior has been determined. In much the same way, the determinists of the current century view all behavior as being determined either by your genes or by the accident of your birth.

WE ARE ALL JUST VICTIMS

Biologists see our innate ability being determined by genes, just as hair color and bone structure are. The beginnings of psychology had their roots in such thinking. Galton sought to show why great composers begot great composers by arguing for genetic predetermination. Current thinking has been set forth by a number of people but probably got its rebirth with Arthur Jensen's publishing in the *Harvard Educational Review* his theories regarding the heritability of intelligence and black people's supposed intellectual inferiority. Others have joined the biological determinism argument including Hans Eysenck, Richard Hernstein, and William Shockley who advocated paying lower-class people to be neutered.

Just as strong on the other side, are those who view people as being products of their environment. There but for the grace of God, go I is their thinking. The only reason that I am not a murderer, rapist, or arsonist has to do with the luck of my environment. The man who goes crazy and shoots up a community is not to blame. He is the victim. He is the victim of his poor unfortunate past. The child molester is not to blame. He was molested himself.

The naturalists explain behavior in a slightly different manner from the biological determinists, but employ the same overall argument. No one is to be blamed for behavior. There is no free will. People in Los Angeles did not loot and start fires because they wanted to; they were either the product of faulty biology or faulty environment, depending upon your beliefs—two different explanations for the same result. Current research suggests that smoking is biologically determined, as are alcoholism, depression, and various other behaviors. No one is responsible any longer for behavior. The LD child cannot learn because of poor biology or because of poor environment. It matters little. Her lot in life is determined.

PEOPLE ARE CAPABLE OF CHOOSING

I take a wholly different view. I believe that people are capable and that allows me to see things differently. People can change, and free will is alive and well. In *I Ain't Much Baby but I'm All I've Got*, Jess Lair said, "Shame on my parents for what I am today, but shame on me for what I am tomorrow."[1] That is the thinking that is needed in the area of LD. Of course, someone who is introduced to letters and numbers early, who is read to every night, who sees her parents reading is more likely to be able to read easily, but those are not absolute requirements. With a few obvious exceptions, *nearly everyone can learn to read.* It is merely a question of how much effort has been put into the attempt to learn to read. Poor readers seldom spend much time learning to read or reading. Good readers spend a lot of time learning to read and reading.

SYMPTOMS OF A SYSTEM

LD is not a separate problem but a symptom of a system that has rewarded and excused idleness and ignorance. Just as LD has a list of symptoms, so too a poor educational system rewarding the slothful and the lazy is a symptom. Social promotion is as much an indictment of the teachers and the system as is anything else. If you went to the movies and were told that the projector was broken, that no money would be refunded, but you would be allowed to stay in your seat and eat your popcorn, you would be incensed. You would demand your money back. If your child has not learned third-grade math and reading, yet he is promoted since he is too big to stay behind, you go along with it. Minimum competency testing, vocational education, certificates of attendance are all symptoms of the same willingness to accept less. How can a system be allowed to perpetrate such a sham on unsuspecting children?

CHILDREN AND LEARNING

Children are exceptional learners. They learn far more than they get credit for. They learn quickly and readily especially when an older person takes an interest in them. Children respond with delight. When their thoughts and actions are shaped by a thoughtful older person, they can learn nearly anything with patience and time. Most learn readily until it is time to go to school, and then some of them are segregated and labeled. But, even they still learn. They learn that they can't learn, that they are dumb, that if they play dumb, the teachers will expect less and excuse their ignorance. Nonachievement and nonteaching are accepted by both teachers and administrators. Eventually it is accepted by parents. Some parents who fight hard in first grade are exhausted by the end of elementary school and secondary teachers never see them. The only parents secondary teachers see at open house are the parents of bright students. The comments are always the same. The parents we need to see never come. Of course not. They were discouraged from coming when their children were in elementary school.

ALL CHILDREN ARE CAPABLE
OF LEARNING

All children need to be viewed as lovable and capable. If they are seen as being capable, learning will be expected. Reading, the great bugaboo of most underachievers, is not that hard to learn once they get rid of the disabling belief that it is difficult to learn. Reading may be difficult for a three year old to learn, yet even some of them learn to read. More four year olds can read, and many more five year olds. By six years of age, most children in the United States are reading at least at a first-grade level. If your child didn't learn how to read at a first grade level by age seven or eight, she probably learned something else. She probably learned that reading was difficult and that she was incapable of learning how to read.

Many of the three, four, and five year olds who can read were taught by an older brother or sister, by their parents, or even by themselves by puzzling out sounds. No one with an advanced degree was needed. No specialist with unique training, just an eight-year-old sister. A teacher (whether sister, mother, or classroom teacher) must believe in a child's capacity to learn, or she won't really even try to teach. What would be the point? Kids desire to learn and learn many new things every day. One study found that young children were learning an average of twenty new words a day. Most educators would claim that that is impossible; that children never even learn ten new vocabulary words a week when they are assigned them. But, I bet you would be hard pressed to find a child of seven or eight who does not know what a condom is. Did he learn what it was in school? No, he learned it from television and interacting with his peers. Unfortunately, the current school system, like most bureaucracies, is concerned with the smooth and efficient running of the schools rather than with good instruction. Administrators wish to maintain the status quo and to get the paperwork in on time.

PRACTICING FOR SUCCESS

When a basketball coach sees his team lose a game because they missed foul shots in the final minute, what does he do? He emphasizes foul shooting in practice. He gets his players to the foul line, instructs them, has them practice, and expects that they will improve. My high school coach would not let us leave the gym at night until we had made ten foul shots in a row. Our foul shooting improved if we wanted to leave.

Vicki Goetz was a phenom on the golf course even in junior high school. By the time she was in high school, she had played with the LPGA touring pros and beaten some of them. Since she was so young her body had not matured so that she could hit the ball as far as the lady pros, but most of the pros she played claim that Vicki is second to none in her short game ability, such as putting and chipping. Vicki claims that she has always stressed the short game in her practice and will not leave the practice green until she makes 100 putts in a row from 6 feet. Most high school golfers don't even make 100 practice putts in a year. No wonder Vicki is head and shoulders above the rest.

A NOTE FROM THE DOCTOR

What do we require of children who have difficulty reading? Do they get more reading, or less? Do we expect them to learn to read or do we make excuses for them and allow them to avoid reading? Do we think a good coach can turn someone into a good free throw shooter by requiring her to shoot free throws? Of course. Do we think someone can turn a poor reader into a good one by requiring him to read? The answer is all too obvious—no, we do not think that. We think that there is something wrong with the child. Leave him alone. Don't put pressure on him. He was predestined to be a poor reader by his heredity or his environment. We might just as well pin a note to his shirt "Please excuse Johnny from reading. His doctor (or psychologist or teacher) determined he is not capable of reading." We then excuse him from learning to read for the rest of his life.

NOTE

1. Lair, J. (1985). *I Ain't Much Baby, but I'm All I've Got*. New York: Faucett.

13

Readiness—Rush to Judgment

An expert is a person who avoids the small errors
as he sweeps on to the grand fallacy.
Benjamin Stolberg

When teachers or parents are puzzled by a child's seeming inability to learn, they frequently seek the advice of an expert. Experts usually take the form of psychologists, psychiatrists, learning diagnosticians, and speech therapists who screen and test for defects in psycholinguistic abilities, memory, perception, and intelligence. The idea is to catch the problem early to provide remediation. The unfortunate outcome of such psychological pokes and probes is the creation of the expectation on everybody's part, including the child, that there is indeed a disability. The problem is that regardless of the outcome of the testing, the children are thought of by the adults in their lives as being disabled learners. Teachers and parents have learned that difference is abnormality. Some revert to other explanations that still leave the child's will out of the configuration. Readiness is one such concept often used to justify lack of school achievement.

READINESS

Readiness is a concept much like intelligence, tallness, attractiveness, and most other human attributes. It is a made-up term used to describe a state. There is no readiness anymore than there is tallness, attractiveness, or cleanliness. They are all characterizations used to describe where someone stands in relationship to others. The concept of readiness is helpful if we see it for what it really is—a description of how ready a child is to learn a certain concept or task. It is not immutable. Just because a child may not have all of the benefits another child has had does not mean he is not ready to learn. In fact, nearly all children learn and learn rapidly.

ALL CHILDREN ARE READY TO LEARN

Herbert Ginsberg in *The Myth of the Deprived Child* asserts that poor children's environment and intellectual development are adequate for promoting the basic forms of cognitive activity.[1] That is, they are ready to learn new things because they have been adequately stimulated by their environment. There are shapes and colors and objects in the poor homes just as there are in middle-class homes. The parents speak; the children listen to television and develop speech patterns very similar to middle class speech patterns, despite the variance with standard English. Ginsberg cites Labov's studies of black speech patterns to assert that black inner-city children's speech patterns are as consistent and predictable as middle-class children's speech patterns.

The most noticeable part of black inner city speech is the difference in the use of the verb be. In black speech, the so-called copula, or helping verb, is often omitted in informal speech, such as "You crazy." Labov concludes that whenever standard English can contract the copula, such as "You're crazy," black speech can omit the copula. The point of Ginsberg's treatise is that poor children develop the cognitive universals and distinctive skills that are useful in their own environment, but are not necessarily useful in schools. That is, while the middle-class child is being read to, given crayons and chalkboards, and singing the ABCs, many children of the working poor are not. Ginsberg concludes:

> General experience with the world—contact with the universal environment of things and people—provides the poor child with the basic intellectual skills of language, concrete operational thinking, and all the other cognitive universals. And yet general experience is not sufficient for the development of some special skills, namely reading and writing, that the school requires. For reading and writing to develop, the child needs a literate environment. Given it, he will learn the fundamentals of reading.[2]

Much the same can be said of the so-called LD youngster. By definition, the LD child has the necessary cognitive ability to read, but, for some reason, she is not able to learn reading and writing at the same time or at the same speed as many of her classmates. I believe that in many cases it has to do with experiences with print prior to school. Just as a child is going to be a complete dunce at playing baseball if he has never held a bat before Little League so, too, is the child who has had no experience with print going to appear to be a dunce at reading. Being a golfer, I frequently hear older golfers wishing they had taken up the sport when they were younger so that they could have developed a good swing. They believe that the golf swing must be learned at some preadolescent age. Larry Nelson, winner of several PGA events including the U.S. Open, may disagree since he did not begin playing golf until 21 years of age. Just as most older amateurs do not take lessons and do not actively seek to improve, poor readers do not take lessons and do not seek to improve. That which I can do, I do; that which I cannot do, I don't. As others progress, I stay the same or progress more slowly. Thus, I fall farther and farther behind my peers even though I may have made gains.

FALSE ASSUMPTIONS ABOUT LEARNING

Again, borrowing from Ginsberg, compensatory education programs are built on certain assumptions. The assumptions are (a) that some children come to school from an inadequate environment; (b) that the environment is the major determinant of the child's intellectual growth; (c) that, as a result, some children develop deficient intellectual skills; and (d) that schools should be designed to remove and correct intellectual deficits. Although Ginsberg is talking about poor children, it requires very little imagination to apply what he is saying to any child having difficulty in school. The slow-learning child is little different from the labeled LD child.

In compensatory programs, children are tracked almost from the outset. Some are even screened before coming to kindergarten so that they can be provided with early intervention. PL 99-457 provides programs beginning at birth for anyone at-risk of being handicapped. The usual school programs for thought-to-be LD students may begin as early as three years of age. The students are given tasks to complete that are often called readiness tasks. Others come to kindergarten or first grade and are instantly put into the lower track and given readiness activities. Those activities frequently consist of finding the different shape in a row of three squares and a circle. Shapes and puzzles are given as prereading activities instead of reading to the child. What happens is that the very children who need the most reading instruction frequently receive the least. Some teachers presume that Johnny is going to have difficulty reading. They say, "Just look at the family he came from," and "His three brothers all had trouble," and, "The father doesn't know how to read," and on and on.

The child is blamed right off the bat. He is underprepared or from an inadequate gene pool. The assumption is incorrect and contributes to the child's continued delays in reading achievement. Only if the child is seen as being infinitely ready and capable can real learning take place. When people ask how Marva Collins is so able to influence children to read when others have not, it is the assumption she starts with that makes the difference. She begins by believing that all children are capable of learning.

When those same people argue for early interventions, they are saying that getting a good foundation is necessary for good reading ability. They dismiss the fact that what happens on a daily basis is far more important than any program. A potential LD student who has a good-second grade teacher will do well. Given a bad teacher, she will do poorly. Schools are so poor in their ability to remediate weaknesses because of the very fact that they believe in weaknesses instead of abilities. Every child must be viewed as being capable for real learning to occur. When compensatory education fails, the belief is that we did not get them early enough. Legislation seeks to correct that by continually reducing the age at which children enter Head Start and similar programs. Soon we will be putting nurseries in public schools or even meeting parents at the hospital so we can take their infants before the parents damage their ability to learn. If that fails, then we will probably start controlling the conditions of pregnancy or start controlling who gets pregnant. If you think that idea is preposterous, remember Schockley and others have suggested paying mothers to get sterilized.

A SUBSTITUTE TEACHER
LEARNS A LESSON

A friend whose wife substituted for a teacher on extended leave, told me the following story: While teaching in an elementary school, his wife made a mistake in assigning one of her students to a reading group by putting him in the top reading group when he had always been in the lowest group. It was several weeks before she learned of her mistake, but by then, the child had done so well, he remained in the top reading group. A mistake in assignment had the fortuitous effect of making the youngster a better reader.

How could a poor reader who was wrongly assigned to the top reading group get so good at reading? Well, several things were probably at work. (a) The substitute teacher not knowing that the boy did not belong in that particular reading group assumed that he was capable of reading at that level and treated him as if he were a good reader. (b) The student probably assumed that he had improved at reading and deserved to be there or he would not have been promoted to the higher level. (c) He also was exposed to better readers and better reading.

It has been shown that teachers treat children who are not good students differently from children who are good students. For example, when calling on students to respond orally, teachers will wait for a longer period of time for a good student than for a poor student, just the opposite of what might be expected. But then, if teachers hold to the assumptions of compensatory education, they believe they are doing right by not embarrassing a poor student any longer than necessary.

IMPORTANCE OF EARLY EXPERIENCES

Few educators or parents doubt the importance of early experiences, but few understand how early experiences work and how diabolical early training can be. First experiences are often decisive in forming children's views. Children who have had a particularly emotional experience, either positive or negative, carry the effects of that experience for years and perhaps a lifetime. The younger a person is, the less intellectually mature and the more powerful the influence of the emotions will be. Early school experiences can shape a child's behavior for life, and many of those experiences are unintentional. A child who, for whatever reasons, is not learning what is being presented is learning many other things—most having to do with her abilities and worthiness regarding those subjects. For example, a boy who has had little exposure to letter sounds and shapes before coming to school may get confused during the first few weeks of instruction. He may carry that confusion with him psychologically from that time on. A student who is unable to perform a certain task, such as letter identification, is not permanently disabled. The skill deficiency is transitory, but his beliefs and feelings about himself may not be transitory. As he becomes older and is better able to cope with letter and sound identification, he may continue to believe that he is incapable of those tasks. He has been programmed to believe that there is something wrong with him. Learning is no longer neutral; it has produced undesired results. The student has learned that he is helpless, dumb, unable to read, a misfit. Henceforth, learning to read will be even more difficult because of that tangential learning. He is like an elephant with a rope around his ankle.

The development of phobias provides a good example of the type of learning I am referring to. Persistent irrational fears are classified by most mental health professionals as being phobias. It is so common in children that phobia is sometimes referred to as the common neurosis of childhood. Books, such as *Your Child from 6 to 12*, list the common fears of each individual age.[3] One of the leading childhood phobias is *school phobia*—a term describing an intense reluctance to go to school. Although some psychologists question its reality, the idea that little children can feel so strongly about school that they refuse to go without protracted intervention is unusual. In just the same way, children can become so frightened of learning that they refuse to participate. Learning is, after all, a participatory adventure, a fact that is often overlooked.

WANTING WHAT IS BEST

Nearly all parents want what is best for their children. They want their children to do well in school, get along with others, prepare for the future, and have fun along the way. From the day a baby is born, parents begin talking to their babies. The more talking the better. They play verbal games with their toddlers, such as, Where is your nose? Where is grandma? See the baby in the mirror.

Some parents begin to teach their children many things early in the belief that it will help them as adults. They want them to know their colors and to sing the alphabet. They may even take them to infant swimming lessons where six-month-old infants are tossed into the water. They often have them begin formal instruction in music, sports, or dance as early as three years of age. Preschool children are taking ballet lessons, suzuki violin, karate, even aerobics. Some parents begin teaching their children to read, often buying books about teaching preschoolers to read. The parents may be pushy but usually in the child's best interest, perhaps with a little parent ego involved.

Many parents spare no expense. Nearly every toy the parents choose has some educational value. Of course, the toys the kids want the experts eschew, like super soakers. Play School and Fisher-Price are offered as the right kinds of toys. Children are put in front of TV sets to watch "Sesame Street," "Electric Company," and "Mr. Rogers Neighborhood" even before they can walk. Although the demand for preschools is growing at a tremendous rate, without an educational component day care centers are avoided. Parents are not sure what is a good educational component or what they want for their children other than some vague notion that children need stimulation to keep up with the Japanese. The media inundate parents with information about what is right and good for children and parents seem to think that they understand. In most respects, parents would say that their children are getting a better start at school than they did. Yet, at the same time we are spending billions in preschool education, more and more children are being identified as handicapped and are being labeled because they need special instruction. In fact, more than two million youngsters have been labeled as LD with several thousand more in preschools waiting to become old enough to receive the label.

BEING DIFFERENT

Being different is now seen as bad, and when a child does anything out of the ordinary, such as not staying seated in a room with rows of desks and a boring lesson, she can be labeled as handicapped. Parents and teachers notice the least little difference and start talking about referrals and testing. Neighbors and relatives offer advice on how to handle those differences. No longer is it okay for children to develop at their own rates since norms tables are used to define disease. A child who falls below a certain point is labeled.

It does not matter that a normal distribution is just that—a *normal* distribution. Most naturally occurring phenomena fall into what is called a normal curve. That does not make the extremes abnormal. Strawberries are raised as a cash crop. People love to buy the largest and reddest berries. Therefore, farmers wishing to increase profits seek to grow and harvest the largest berries they can. People will even pay more for larger berries, but does that make the small berries defective? Are they any less than strawberries because they are smaller? Imagine declaring all berries which fell below the fifteenth percentile as being so different from other strawberries that they are not capable of being sold. Would that make them any less strawberries? Or any less tasty? Would the farmer producing the small berries not try to sell them? Would any person be willing to pay for small berries? J. M. Smuckers Company would certainly buy the small berries and turn them into jams and jellies. No one would know their size then. The differences in size are minor. The essence of being a berry is always with them. And so it is with LD children. The essence of being human is always with them. The differences among children are minor.

MAKING CHILDREN HANDICAPPED

The LD label carries with it significant consequences for the children so labeled. Children who are labeled as LD are, in effect, declared to be so different from other children that they are not capable of learning. They are moved to separate classes, parents are informed about their children's handicap, and expectations are set. If people believe what they are told, they tend to become what they are called. Call your children disabled often enough, and they will prove you right, especially if experts are the ones doing the labeling. Remember that with some bending of the rules or stretching of the criteria (if there are any) almost any child can be labeled as LD. The criteria are like rubber rulers; they can be stretched to meet any requirement.

The idea that small classes could help remediate child's problems seems kind enough at first blush but the help does not seem to help. So-called average youngsters are not being returned to regular classes after being fixed. Instead, they continue on the downward spiral associated with being called defective, becoming more and more engulfed as they no longer seek to improve.

ENGULFED IN THE LD SYNDROME

I must refer back to the story of Josh in chapter 7 who was identified as being LD in seventh grade after earning a score in spelling that was fifteen points below his IQ score. The Wide Range Achievement Test (WRAT) was used. It is called "the rat," and that is just what it is when in the wrong hands. Jerome Sattler, who has written a respected text entitled *Assessment of Children*, cautions about the limitations of the WRAT with the following: "[The] limitations mean that the test should be used in a cautious manner and only for screening—not for diagnostic placement decisions."[4]

Well, the wrong hands used the WRAT to place Josh in an LD class. Fifteen points below the IQ score was the minimum criterion for being called LD. In no other subjects were his standard scores fifteen points below his IQ. So based on one spelling test of forty-six words that can place a student from nursery school to college level, this student was given the label of learning disabled. No matter that experts like Sattler caution against using the WRAT for placement decisions. No matter that in all other subject areas he was achieving within the safe range of less that fifteen standard score points. No matter that he had been tested at least twice during elementary school and was not found eligible for LD services. He was now declared LD by a team of experts. That is all it takes to become LD, declaration by experts.

The federal government says that there must be a severe discrepancy between IQ and achievement for a student to be called LD, but many states do not quantify what a severe discrepancy is or use minimal criteria, such as an achievement score which is one standard deviation below IQ or two grade levels below placement. Josh scored one standard deviation below IQ only on a spelling test. Most LD experts would insist on more evidence before declaring a child LD, but the decisions about who is called LD rest with the local bureaucrats who bend the rules to suit their fancy. It is interesting that Josh was never called LD all during elementary school, but after failing one spelling test in seventh grade, he miraculously became LD. More tragic, however, in less than six months, he was in LD for all academic subjects. He was even placed in LD for math because he was failing math in the regular class even though his math scores were well above his IQ score.

DOING THE CHILD A FAVOR

Overzealous professionals believe that they are doing the child and her parents a favor by providing special programs. They think that the child will receive a better education and more individual attention with such a label. That belief has led many professionals to take liberties with the law and to place many students in LD who might not otherwise be eligible. I read one psychological report that called a student an overachieving LD youngster since his achievement scores were above his grade placement. What evidence did the psychologist cite for the boy being LD in the first place? Hair whorls in the wrong direction and a medical history which included a difficult labor for his mother.

Once children are placed into special education, even for part of the day, they can get further behind in their regular classes. Not only that, the regular education teachers begin to view them differently. Josh was seen as not being a capable student any longer when he was placed in special education. As the regular education teachers came to learn of Josh's disability, they began to excuse his failure to do work in their classes. Josh was willing to take the easy road and no longer did any school work. He became LD by default.

Special education teachers also promote the helplessness syndrome of LD students by doing work for them. Not only do some special teachers no longer require adequate work, they excuse inadequate work; they copy notes, assignments, and, in some cases, actually writing papers and homework assignments for their students. Many parents are guilty of similar behavior. Those methods make students more dependent on teachers and parents instead of less dependent.

Of course, some LD students do improve in school but that is rarely the result of some insight gained by the testing and the subsequent label applied. Quite often, it is the result of a desire to please, an inability to get away with not doing work, or a desire to get out of a special class. What we need to do is to study the few successful LD students to learn why they were successful. Usually, it is from hard work, something antithetical to the excuse making most LD students endure. Plain old good teaching with high expectations and hard work is what will overcome reading failure.

NOTES

1. Ginsberg, H. (1972). *The myth of the deprived child*. Englewood Cliffs, NJ: Prentice Hall.

2. Ibid., p. 188.

3. Chilman, C. S. (1966). *Your child from 6 to 12*. Washington, DC: U.S. Government Printing Office.

4. Sattler, J. M. (1988). *Assessment of children*. San Diego: Author.

14

Good Teaching

*The object of teaching a child is to enable
him to get along without his teacher.*
Elbert Hubbard

Maddie Brown was the best classroom teacher I ever had. I have attended some seminars with truly great teachers, for which I paid dearly, but Maddie Brown was an everyday high school math teacher in a small high school in western New York state. Madeline Brown was the only math teacher for grades nine through twelve. She taught algebra, plane geometry, trigonometry, solid geometry, and calculus. Every student knew her reputation as a no nonsense teacher, and every student came to her class anticipating hard work. There was no fooling around. I never remember her digressing into some esoteric discussion so she would not have to teach. She was all business. David Butts found out the first day of algebra class and nearly every day thereafter. Whenever someone did not know how to do a problem, answer a question, or did not have his homework completed, Mrs. Brown merely said, "After school," and began writing out a pass for detention. Everyone knew that you had to stay if she said that phrase, and you would stay until you knew the answers and had your homework completed for the next day. Some, including David Butts, stayed nearly every night, usually for a couple of hours.

There were few jokes in Mrs. Brown's classroom. There wasn't time. There was little laughter, yet it was not a somber place. Mrs. Brown was always happy. She enjoyed math and enjoyed getting students to learn what they thought they could not learn. She expected the best and was satisfied with nothing less from every student. A detention note from Mrs. Brown was like a life sentence. She would keep her eye on that person forevermore.

Poor David Butts. He stayed after school more that anyone I have ever met, yet, more important, he passed algebra. There never was any question that he would pass. You see, every student passed Mrs. Brown's mathematics classes eventually. She wouldn't let anyone fail.

A NOT-SO-GOOD TEACHER

One of the reasons I remember Mrs. Brown so well was that I moved to another school district for my senior year. In that school, I had another math teacher, one who probably knew as much math as Mrs. Brown, but one who knew nothing of teaching and how to get students to work. I took solid geometry and calculus at the new school. Only four students signed up for those courses. I played football and basketball, worked part time in the evenings, and was in the class play so I had a busy schedule. I seldom did my math homework because I was so busy and because the teacher never required it, expected it, or even asked to check it. The four of us would sit in class and talk, copying each other's homework and getting the teacher to talk about other things so that we would not have to work. My grades showed the difference in teachers, too. My average for the year in math was 80 percent. On the State Regents Examination, I scored a 75 percent, barely passing, yet I received the award for the highest average in math and science for four years in my graduating class. How? Because of the extremely high grades I received from Mrs. Brown. I usually had grades of 97 percent or higher, yet at the new school I had become below average. I turned into a lazy student who previously was the class whiz in a difficult subject. Do not misinterpret what I am saying here. Of course, I was responsible for my grades, but when I was allowed to goof off, I did. When I had a teacher who insisted on the best from everyone and who expected nothing less, I was an excellent math student. When I had a teacher who allowed me and others to get away with minimal effort, I was a terrible math student.

OTHER GOOD TEACHERS

Jaime Escalante is a hero in many educational circles. Escalante is the high school teacher in Los Angeles who taught calculus to inner-city students who were not supposed to do well in mathematics. Escalante's story was depicted in the film *Stand*

and Deliver. Escalante believes that the sole concern of teachers should be to help students. He spends his lunch hour and time before and after school tutoring students who need help. He spends his free time calling parents to enlist their support and to gain community support. He sounds a lot like Mrs. Brown.

In West Chester, Pennsylvania, Remo Ciccone is a teacher who fashions himself after Escalante. According to a report in the *Philadelphia Inquirer*, Ciccone's philosophy is, "Set impossibly high standards, and students will rise to meet them. Although some students may sink initially under pressure, passion and dedication can work miracles."

Both Ciccone and Escalante have had great success in preparing their students for the advanced Placement Calculus Examination. They expect much and get it. That is much the same philosophy that Marva Collins has employed in teaching inner city youth in Chicago. Collins, who wrote *The Marva Collins Way*, took the rejects of Chicago schools and turned them into high achieving students by constantly having high expectations for students who had never before been expected to learn. Other people's expectations seem to have a great deal to do with what we learn.

When we call young children LD, we are condemning them to a life of limited expectations. Parents, teachers, and the children themselves come to expect little and are seldom disappointed. How many LD students, if they had teachers like Maddie Brown, Jaime Escalante, or Marva Collins would no longer be LD? The labeling itself produces expectations and perceptions of failure.

A woman who was institutionalized as a youngster vowed never to allow anyone she had a chance to help to get away with lowered expectations. That young woman, Annie Sullivan, became the teacher who unlocked the mind of Helen Keller. Sullivan would not allow Keller to get by. Sullivan insisted on high expectations for a child who had been reared more like an animal than a person.

LANGUAGE AND EDUCATION

The language of education is certainly interesting. I am sure that in my years in education and particularly in the years as school psychologist I have been guilty of the obscure statement of the obvious, but I am not sure why we do it. I suppose it has to do with the way we think the words will be perceived by others. When things are too obvious they do not even need to be stated, but if we talk in jargon, then the obvious is obscured and we sound all-knowing. Sending schoolwork home in a folder so the parents can see it is called an intervention. Having a student stay after school is called student management control. A note to the parents is a communication.

This mysticizing of education has produced jargon and beliefs that fly in the face of logic. We can no longer see a child who cannot read for what he is—a child who needs to be taught to read. Reading and math are not all that difficult to learn or to teach. Average parents can, and perhaps should, teach their own children to read and to do math, but our reliance on the experts does not allow us to think such things. If the child does not learn to read quickly, the child must be disabled. There must be some mysterious thing that keeps her from learning. After all, wouldn't she learn if she could?

The only conclusion we can make when we cut through this gibberish is that the child is at fault. He has learning problems. He is an underachiever. He is handicapped, disabled, or disturbed. The result is that education professors create little empires studying what they announce to be important. Students who are not inner directed, don't learn. Neuromuscular functioning is not adequate. Visual perception is suspect. Attention deficits are at fault. The child is somehow inadequate.

YOU DON'T NEED AN EXPERT
TO TEACH READING

There are plenty of books on teaching reading at home. Thousands, perhaps millions, of children have learned to read at home. The average person who can read can teach someone else to read. It takes no special training. If I can teach you to golf, dribble a basketball, or play the violin, I can also teach you to read. Reading is a skill, and, as with any skill, practice and the right instruction improve performance. How did people learn to read before schools? Especially before the twentieth-century school with its departmentalized classes and reading groups? The answer is simple. *People taught people to read.* I recently heard a woman on a radio talk show state that there was less illiteracy 100 years ago than there is today. I only heard part of the broad cast and did not get the woman's name so I have no way of knowing whether her facts are correct, but it certainly is an interesting thought. If her facts are correct, it merely lends support to what I have said. The teaching of reading is not some magic performed by educational experts. It is a decoding skill easily taught to most children when they are ready to learn. After all, elementary teachers have no special insight into the teaching of reading. It is as much a mystery to them as it is to you and me, maybe more so because they have been confused by their undergraduate instruction.

The courses they take in college do not make them experts. They dress in funny costumes and read short stories aloud, make colorful bulletin boards, and get As. They do not understand when they are told to make the reading relevant or to enter the local culture of the pluralistic, diverse population that they serve. They are never told that they are responsible for their student's learning.

What is taught in teacher training programs has little to do with content. It has to do with feeling good, motivation, relevancy, and the like. Prospective teachers are taught about the different handicaps but are never taught how to teach children with those handicaps.

TEACHING YOUR CHILD TO READ

If there were no schools, would you be able to teach your own child to read? What if there were no reading series, no books on how to teach reading? Could you still do it? Let's face it. Of course, you could. There is no magic formula. I dare say you could do it far better and quicker than the nonsense that goes on in schools. You would probably never give your child a series of workbook sheets. You would probably sit down and read to him and have him follow along. You would teach him that a makes an /a/ sound as in apple, that b makes a /b/ sound as in bat, that c makes a /k/ sound as is cat, and so on. You would teach him that some letters make two sounds a also sounds like /ay/ as in gate, c also sounds like /s/ as in circus, and so on. You would drill and practice and keep telling him until he understood. You would keep reading to him, stopping occasionally to ask him what sound a letter makes. Gradually, you would ask him to do more and more of the sounding out until he was reading comfortably. You would introduce him to books which are written for his age and ability and which he would enjoy. That is all it takes to teach reading. You do not need a specialist with an advanced degree. Anyone, even a peer can teach reading if he has mastered it.

Writing is, after all, a code—little symbols on a page that have a meaning because of agreement. Teach someone the code, and they can read. At first, they may sound out words, but eventually they will read whole words. They will come to learn that the letters h, o, u, s, e spell *house*. They will not have to sound it out every time. No matter in what type the letters are set, or whether they are printed, written, scrawled or scribbled, they will always spell house. That is not a hard concept to teach any normal youngster above the age of six or seven. It can easily be learned by children much younger and can be learned by students with below average IQ scores.

In *In Search of the IQ Correlation, A Scientific Whodunit*, a teacher not knowing any better tried to teach reading to a group of mentally retarded youngsters using a system of reading called Ball-Stick-Bird.[1] I say the author did not know any better because she tried to teach reading to students who most special educators would tell her were too low-functioning to learn reading; that little should be expected academically from the retarded; that they might be able to learn to identify caution and danger signs such as Don't Walk and No Smoking; but that they really can't learn to read beyond a primarily level.

Fortunately, the author did not know that and taught very low-functioning students to read at a fourth- or fifth-grade level, about the reading level of most newspapers. The teacher taught the students a simple code. The students learned the code and decoded the stories.

READING IS DECODING

That's all reading is—decoding. Lots of people argue that reading is more than decoding that it is comprehension which, of course, it is not. They will argue that it does no good to be able to decode if you cannot understand what you are reading. With that I may agree, but it takes one giant leap of ignorance to say that someone is not reading if she can identify words. This read you can? Does the preceding sentence make sense? No? Well, did you read it? If you can identify the words you have read it. It does not matter that you cannot comprehend it. Given the right information, you can comprehend it. The sentence was merely presented in backwards order. Turn the words around—can you read

This?—and it makes sense. Would anyone argue that reading the four words in backwards order is not reading but reading them in forward order is reading. I hope not.

Reading is cracking a code. Once children are taught the code, they can read. The code is not that difficult to learn, maybe forty-five different sounds and a few different spellings of those sounds. One can refine his reading ability as he becomes familiar with it—just as one can refine a golf swing. You do not have to know how to draw or fade a ball to be able to play golf. Some people never learn how, yet are above-average golfers. They may refine their skills enough to be able to do it, but it is not necessary. Nor is it necessary to be able to read long words and confusing passages to be able to read.

CONDEMNING CHILDREN
TO BE NONREADERS

Teach a child the basic code and the ability to sound out words using that code, and she can read. Experience and practice will make her a better reader, but she will always be a reader. When I was a school psychologist, I was amazed by the number of teachers and parents who would condemn a child to the category of nonreader based on their narrow pronouncements. Johnny can't read so the referral forms would read. Sometimes there were qualifications, such as Johnny is a virtual nonreader. Even though I tested more than 1,500 students referred to me for academic problems, I never saw a child of average ability over the age of eight who could not read. He might not be able to identify all, or even most of the words on a typical sight word reading list, but he could read some of them. He had some skill in reading. He had the ability to decipher some of the codes. Instead of building on those strengths, the teachers condemned him to a life of non-reading by conferring the status of nonreader on him. With the status of nonreader, he no longer needed to try to learn. No effort was needed. He was off the hook.

LIMITING TEACHERS' EFFECTIVENESS

Teachers respond to what they have come to believe about reading based on the teacher training programs and the experiences they have observed. I would dare say that there are few school districts in America that have not adopted a reading series from which all teachers are required to teach reading. Teachers limit their reading instruction to the activities presented in those series. Reading is confined to the morning. Then the rest of the day, the teacher teaches math, social studies, science, handwriting, and so on. Reading is left in the reading block of time in the morning when we know all children are born to learn to read. Move reading to the afternoon and teachers rebel. "You know that I have to have reading in the morning when the kids are fresh." I guess it is okay to teach social studies or science to stale kids.

WHEN IS A TEACHER A TEACHER?

Parents don't need any special dispensation from the schools to teach reading to their children. Teachers don't need any dispensation either if they are truly teachers, but many of them are not. Not in the real sense. If a person in front of a classroom presents information and no one learns it, is the person a teacher? If I were to try to teach about the American Revolution to a group of youngsters who could not speak English, and none of them understood what I had said, would I be a teacher? Of course not. However, if I could find a way to teach by bringing in an interpreter, using audiovisual materials, and maps and pictures, and if they got a sense of the Boston Tea Party, the battle of Bunker Hill, and so on, would I then be a teacher? Of course. Well, too many of today's teachers present material and forget about the children. One educator, tongue-in-cheek, said that he had taught his child to swim, but every time the kid got into the pool he went to the bottom. That is how some teachers view teaching. They did the teaching, the children just didn't get it.

THE BEST INSTRUCTION I EVER RECEIVED

I remember when I was in fourth grade. On a Friday, our teacher gave us a test on multiplication facts. When the tests were graded and returned, I found that I had missed nearly all of the nines facts. I remember what happened after we got those tests back as clearly as if it were yesterday. The girl sitting next to me, Nancy Hinton, asked me how I had done. I told her that I had done well, except for the nines; they were really hard. Nancy was surprised and told me that nines were the easiest to remember. How could they be easy? Ones were easy; twos were easy; fives were easy, but when you got up to the sixes, sevens, and eights they were hard. Nines must be the hardest of all. Whatever did Nancy mean by saying that the nines were easy? Fortunately, I was curious enough to ask, and Nancy told me.

"Don't you remember Mrs. Carl telling us about adding the digits to get nine?"

I had no idea what she was talking about. She then did some of the best teaching I have ever encountered. She did a one-time teaching lesson that has stuck with me to the present time.

"You know," Nancy continued. "Mrs. Carl taught us, 'two times nine is eighteen. The one and eight add up to nine. Three times nine is twenty-seven. The two and seven add up to nine. Four times nine is thirty-six. The three and six add up to nine. Each time you take one from the back digit and add it to the front digit to get the answer. Thus, you take one from the six in thirty-six and add it to the three and you would get forty-five. The next would be fifty-four and the next sixty-three, seventy-two, and eighty-one. Just keep taking one from the back digit and adding it to the front digit. Take one from nine (9 x 1) and put it in front and you will have eighteen. The two digits always add up to nine."

I saw it immediately. The sum of the digits of the answers added up to nine every time. I never again had to learn the nines tables. I knew them instantly. I asked Nancy how she knew about the nines tables since I had never heard the teacher tell us about them. Nancy told me that the nines had been taught the previous week. Then, I remembered. I had missed one day of school when I was sick the previous week. It was rare for me to miss school, but I had apparently missed the one day we covered the nines tables. I had not had the opportunity to learn the nines. It was good instruction by a peer that taught me in a one-time lesson about the nines tables, and it is good teaching that will keep children from being labeled with disabling names such as LD.

NOTE

1. Fuller, R. (1977). *In search of the IQ correlation: A scientific whodunit.* Stony Brook, NY: Ball-Stick-Bird Publications.

15

What Really Is LD?

Nothing is right or wrong but thinking makes it so.
Shakespeare

If you have read the first fourteen chapters, you know I think LD is a labeling process that is expedient and downright harmful. The idea is that the child does not fit. It is somehow the child's fault, or the fault of his genes, background, or parents that he is not learning in school. The child is seen as different and somehow diseased. Of course, no one can tell you how or to what degree, but nearly every book on LD begins with a chapter of definitions citing the challenge in defining LD. The books usually conclude that it is impossible to arrive at an acceptable definition but that children still have difficulties in school and, therefore, still have learning disabilities.

I contend that *LD is the product of the institutions in which the children must deal rather than something within the children themselves.* That idea is not new or unique. An example of such thinking is the following:

> A learning-disabled child is neither damaged nor permanently impaired. The disability is an inability to make use of the unspecialized instruction usually found in the typical classroom. Given proper and specialized instruction, the disability disappears. The problem is thus an *educational problem* [italics added], not a psychological problem or a medical problem. The responsibility for helping these children ultimately rests with the educators, for a learning disability is not so much a lack in the child's ability to learn as *it is a lack in the educator's ability to identify and teach children with special educational needs* [italics added].[1]

This view of LD as being primarily an educational problem has been talked about in the literature for years. In fact, the previous quote is from 1977. Yet, the notion that the average person has (and it might be added, the notion that the average teacher has) dates back to the early supposing about LD. The notion formulated back then was that LD children are *minimally* brain damaged or that they have learning disabilities. Scott Sigmon addresses the notion that the general public has with the following:

> Obviously, there are people with brain damage who have concomitant learning problems; but the theory that connects brain damage to LD without hard medical substantiation is often flawed...the major catastrophe has been the massive expansion of the (formally labeled) LD student population by workers with good intent who, unfortunately, greatly expanded the ideas [of LD].[2]

PROBLEMS IN SCHOOLING

The idea of the institution causing the disease has not been applied to only education. Thomas Szasz suggested that mental illness is a myth and might better be described as a problem in living and much of the treatment of mental illness merely exacerbates the problem.[3] Along that same vein, I see LD as a problem in schooling and most of the remedies we provide exacerbate the problem. Some children have problems in school, just as some adults have problems in living. In fact, the number of children who are having difficulty in school seems to be growing, yet viewing the problem as being within the child is downright detrimental. Mistaking constructs for facts has led many to make incorrect conclusions about children.

For example, when a kindergarten teacher or parent sees a student writing letters in reverse, the thinking is that there is something wrong with the child—a potential LD child. And why shouldn't a teacher or parent have such a belief? They have been indoctrinated with the dogma of disease. They believe, as do most others, that if the child can't learn, the child, her genes, or her medical history is at fault. In the original supposing about LD, letter reversals were seen as symptoms of LD. The kindergarten teacher long ago learned that reversing letters in reading and writing is a symptom of LD, and she becomes concerned when she encounters it. Has the belief about letter reversals as a symptom of learning problems ever been substantiated? No. In fact, it has been demonstrated that *reversals are a normal part of learning and may occur in good readers more often than in bad readers.* Do you suppose that the average kindergarten teacher or the average parent has any indication of that?

In *The Learning Mystique*, a book that does a brilliant job of locating and exposing the myths surrounding LD, Gerald Coles spends much time discussing the lack of evidence regarding reversals and most of the other beliefs about LD.[4] I refer you to his book if you wish further information. His debunking is thorough and complete. What do his critics say of his exposure of the facts? They claim that the facts are old stuff; that people in the field have known for years that reversals are not an indication of LD. Never mind that few teachers or parents know that. The critics attack Coles for telling what is already known, even if it is only known to a select few. One expert responding to Coles book, admitted that he had not read the book and did not wish to.[5] I guess he did not want to be confused by facts.

LD IS NOT DICHOTOMOUS

People believe that LD is an actual disease, but LD is not like cancer. In cancer tests, the results come back either malignant or not malignant. There is a dichotomy, either you have it or you don't. You cannot confirm LD with an either/or test. It is a matter of degree just like tallness or baldness. I am 6 feet 1 inches tall. In high school, I was a center on the basketball team and as tall as anyone in my rural graduating class of 41 students. Many times during my life, people have referred to me as tall. What standards did they use to determine that I was tall? Any standards they wanted to use. Tallness is subjective. Imagine you are in charge of dividing the population into tall and short? What standards would you choose? If you chose 7 feet as the cutoff for tall, no one would argue that anyone above 7 feet is tall, but then the person who is 6 feet 11 inches would not be tall—how preposterous. As the cutoff is lowered, more people would be included as tall, but even more would just miss the cutoff. For example, if the cutoff were set at 6 feet 7 inches, then more 6 foot 6 inch people would be excluded from being tall than there would have been excluded at 6 feet 11 inches.

What about short? Is 5 feet short? Is 5 feet 2 inches short? If so, 5 feet 2 1/4 inches becomes average. Of course, we could have several levels of shortness, such as mildly short, moderately short, and severely short just like we do with mental retardation. All we would succeed in doing in that scenario is to create more cutoffs that people barely miss or make.

LD IS A MATTER OF DEGREE

Just as labeling someone as tall or short is a matter of degree, labeling someone as LD is also a matter of degree. This changing of degree depending upon where you are and who is doing the determining is a frightening proposition, yet that is exactly what happens with LD youngsters. Eligibility comes down to splitting hairs. In one state or school district a child is not LD, in another he is.

In an appeals case recently determined in Pennsylvania, even the experts could not agree as to what constitutes LD. Bethany was determined not to be LD by the school district psychologist. The parents took Bethany to an independent psychologist who determined that Bethany was LD. When the school district did not honor the other psychologist's determination and would not call Bethany LD, the parents requested a due process hearing. The hearing officer sided with the parents' psychologist who had determined that the girl was LD. Upon appeal to the Commonwealth Appeals Review Panel, it was determined that Bethany was not LD. Eligibility criteria for LD is so indeterminate that no one can decide in individual cases if it is really being applied correctly. Two psychologists looking at the same data could not agree. Two independent administrative decisions regarding the same data produced two different determinations. Who is correct? Whoever gets the final say. Similar scenarios of disagreement occur almost daily across the United States. It is difficult in individual cases to determine eligibility, and the determinations almost always are based on the biases of the determiners.

EVIDENCE AGAINST LD

The most damning indictment against LD is that there is no accepted body of evidence to confirm even the existence of LD, much less how to treat it. The problem is that once LD has been accepted into the popular beliefs of the culture, trying to disprove its existence is nearly impossible. Can anyone disprove the existence of UFOs, ghosts, or Bigfoot? No matter how much evidence one gathers regarding the nonexistence of something, believers will say "Yes, but," believing that circumstantial evidence constitutes proof. In like fashion, you can never disprove the existence of LD because LD really means whatever an adult doesn't like. The adult may be a teacher, a psychologist, or even a parent, but since the symptoms are drawn from a laundry list in which such diverse things as hair whorls, hurting the family cat, and stealing cars can be accepted as proof of LD, nearly anyone can cite symptoms and assert existence of the condition.

RONNIE

I evaluated a student named Ronnie while he was in a departmentalized sixth grade. Ronnie had five different teachers, none of whom believed he was having any difficulty in school. In fact, Ronnie was an A student in all subjects but math in which he got Bs. The evaluation was conducted at the parent's request. They complained of Ronnie's behavior at home. He would come home from school, throw his books across the room, and yell at his elderly parents. The parents, who were in their 60s, believed that Ronnie's behavior was the result of pent up frustration from school that he had to release when he got home.

Following the evaluation, I explained to Ronnie's parents that he was above average in intelligence and was doing well in all academic areas. There was no indication of any educational problems. I suggested that they tell Ronnie firmly and directly that he was no longer to throw his books or yell at them. The father told me that I was wrong, that there clearly was something wrong with Ronnie, and asked if I would please call Ronnie handicapped even if he did not need special education classes. You see, Ronnie's brothers and sisters were grown and had children of their own and were criticizing how their parents handled Ronnie. The parents insisted that there was something wrong with Ronnie so they could excuse his behavior. He could not be made to stop throwing his books and yelling if he was disabled. They believed that he was LD, even if he was an A student. Why did they believe so strongly? They did not want to be responsible for his outbursts and saw LD as a convenient excuse because it has been sold so well.

LD IS ABSURD

The concept of learning disability is absurd. LD theory suggests that someone can have a disability to learn certain things in certain situations yet can later learn those same things with little trouble. It asserts that some children cannot sit still, discriminate visually, listen attentively, or do thousand of other things most children can do. Yet, those same children can demonstrate those very skills of sitting still, discriminating visually, or listening attentively and those behaviors are over-looked. In reality, labeling children as LD is no more than an administrative convenience. It is legislatively approved segregation under the guise of helping children. However laudable the intentions of the legislature or of the professionals providing the programs, children are not helped. They are, of course, removed from the regular teacher's hair, which makes regular education teachers strong proponents of LD classes.

Another problem with LD classification has to do with differences in children's performances being highly exaggerated. Just like with tallness, whenever a cutoff is established for something, many people are near the cutoff, just barely making it or missing it. A child may be declared to be LD if her achievement test scores are more than one standard deviation below her IQ score, usually a fifteen point difference. An IQ score of 100 and a reading standard score of 85, may allow a child to be placed in LD, yet getting one more question right on an achievement test may boost a first grader's standard score from 85 to 93 which is in the normal range.[6] The question may be something as simple as identifying a curved line, a concept that, if missed, may be taught to the student and she may never miss it again. But, children are labeled based on the scores without consideration of what tasks were missed or if they could be easily learned.

EFFICACY STUDIES

Even if the concept of LD is absurd, I would not be so adamant in my denigration if children were being helped in LD classes, but they are not being helped. Recently, I submitted to a professional journal an article critical of LD. The article was rejected at least partially because of my claim that LD interventions were not helpful. One of the reviewers rejected my article because he felt that many parents and students could be found who would testify to the benefit of LD classes. Although testimony is sometimes enlightening, the reviewer's opinion falls short on at least two counts—(a) there is no single, overwhelming voice extolling the virtues of LD placement and (b) individual testimony is little more than personal accounts similar to extolling the virtues of snake oil. Regarding the first point, if LD were truly the boon it is supposed to be, much evidence would be available to support the testimony of the parents and there would be an avalanche of good press. On the contrary, most parents who are supportive of LD programs do so because it has removed the pressure to perform in school or has removed a student from a troublesome teacher. Children are more relaxed but that does not mean the programs have provided benefit beyond respite care.

Regarding the second point, nearly any extreme treatment or method has its true believers. Laetrile, obtained from apricot pits, was supposed to cure cancer. Jim Jones led a large contingent to Jonestown with the promise of a better life. Advocates of psychic healing believe that practitioners really reach inside the human body without benefit of surgery and remove tumors. The *National Enquirer* reports nearly weekly on someone willing to say he encountered a UFO, a ghost, or Bigfoot. Because of just such fanatical claims, individual testimony is viewed with askance in the research community. To have credence, evidence of the effectiveness of programs must be based on research using random samples and subject to all of the other assumptions regarding good research. When special education is looked at under such light, it does not fair well.

Most efficacy studies regarding special education have not been able to demonstrate any advantage for the special placement despite the lower student teacher ratio, special training, and higher costs. In reviewing numerous special education efficacy studies, it was reported that:

> From the studies cited, there is almost universal agreement that the *mentally handicapped children enrolled in special education classes achieve, academically, significantly less than similar children who remain in the regular grades* [italics added]. If the special class groups have any advantage over the regular class groups, it appears to be slight and probably not

particularly meaningful.   This latter finding comes despite the overwhelming evidence of lack of peer accep- tance of the mentally handicapped in the regular classroom. The only area in which the special class has demonstrated superiority of any significance is in peer acceptance.   The mentally handicapped children are more accepted by their mentally handicapped peers in a special class.[7]

Of course, the author is talking about the mentally handicapped, not LD specifically, but both groups are often educated together in mixed category resource classes and integrated into regular classes together. Furthermore, the great decrease in mentally retarded (MR) and concomitant increase in LD since the passage of PL 94-142 obscures many differences between the two groups. Many of today's LD youngsters would have been yesterday's MR youngsters since there is no clear definition of what LD is.

Conrad Carlberg and Kenneth Kavale analyzed fifty primary research studies regarding the efficacy of special education programs and concluded that "special class placement is an inferior alternative to regular class placement in benefiting children removed from the educational mainstream."[8] The con- clusions are hard to escape, but education has been doing a good job of escaping them. LD is a made up term used to get help for children but the benefit of the programs has not been demon- strated.

NOTES

1. Ross, A. O. (1977). *Learning disability the unrealized potential.* New York: McGraw-Hill, p. 11.

2. Sigmon, S. B. (1989). Reaction to excerpts from *The Learning Mystique*: A rational appeal for change. *Journal of Learning Disabilities*, 22(5), p. 298.

3. Szasz, T. S. (1961). *The myth of mental illness.* New York: Harper and Row.

4. Coles, G. (1987). *The learning mystique.* New York: Pantheon.

5. Rourke, B. P. (1989). Coles's learning mystique: The good, the bad, and the irrelevant. *Journal of Learning Disabilities*, 22(5), 274-277.

6. The example was taken from the Peabody Individual Achievement Test using a first-grade math test.

7. Johnson, G. O. (1962). Special education for the mentally handicapped—A paradox. *Exceptional Children, 29,* 62-69.

8. Carlberg, C., & Kavale, K. (1980). The efficacy of special versus regular class placement for exceptional children: A meta-analysis. *The Journal of Special Education,* 14(3), p. 304.

16

Getting Along
in Regular Education

All change is not growth; as all movement is not forward.
Ellen Glasgow

Form L-M of the Stanford Binet Intelligence Scale, contains a question which asks:

> When there is a collision, the last car of the train is usually damaged most. So they have decided that it will be best if the last car is always taken off before the train starts. What is foolish about that?[1]

I hope the answer is obvious to you since the question is expected to be answered correctly by eleven year olds of normal intelligence. But the answer, apparently, is not obvious to the millions of educators who think that if they could just get rid of the bottom students in their classes they would be better able to teach. This last car belief system has resulted in homogeneous grouping of students to promote a more similar group of youngsters—special education being just another version of that system. This last car approach to special education has not been supported by research, yet educators continue to believe that they are doing it for the child's own good.

As more and more LD students are being identified, many are being educated in regular classrooms part of the day and in resource rooms for the remainder of the day. Those so-called pull-out programs are seen as the most effective way of allowing students the opportunity to remain with nonhandicapped peers and still receive the special instruction that they need. This integration with regular education students is called mainstreaming and is based in theory on the requirements of PL 94-142 which mandates that handicapped students be educated in the least restrictive environment (LRE) although the terms *main-*

stream and *mainstreaming* are never specifically mentioned in the law.

Where did this concept of mainstreaming come from then, and what are its implications? Specifically, what did the legislature intend regarding mainstreaming with the passage of 94-142? The law states that special education students should be in the regular classroom to the "maximum extent appropriate." Such terms are left to be defined operationally by the street-level bureaucrats assigned the tasks of working directly with the public. The street-level bureaucrats involved in such definitions in special education are the school building administrators, teachers, and school psychologists involved in the identification and placement of such students.

WHAT IS LRE?

LRE can be viewed as a normalization of the special students' education so that the program in which the student will receive an education is as close as possible to what he would receive if he were not handicapped. If the student is mildly handicapped, then the law requires that:

> handicapped children...are educated with children who
> are not handicapped and that special classes, separate
> schooling, or the removal of handicapped children from
> the regular education environment occurs only when the
> nature or severity of the handicap is such that education
> in regular classes with the use of supplementary aids
> and services cannot be achieved satisfactorily.[2]

It seems clear that the legislature wanted to stop the wholesale removal of large groups of children from regular education. They do not want children removed unless they cannot be helped in regular classes with supplementary aids and services. But, what are supplementary aids and services and how many or how much should be provided before removal from regular classes? Again, the street-level bureaucrats are left to decide.

One of the major problems with the movement toward integration is that it is not coming from regular educators nor even from special education practitioners, but from special education universities. The debate is primarily one group of educators arguing for the status quo (keep special education as it is) while the other group is arguing for a restructuring of regular education to accommodate the so-called mildly handicapped. Both groups are primarily made up of college professors, not practitioners.

The arguments cited against most special education integration models is their lack of empirical evidence. Despite frequent expressions of support for the effectiveness of integration into regular education as a full time, large-scale program, no validation has been based on an independent, systematic, and comprehensive review of empirical evidence. That may be true, but virtually no educational program has ever been implemented on the basis of an independent, systematic, and comprehensive review of empirical evidence. Certainly PL 94-142 which has helped produce the current state of affairs in special education had no such empirical base. The inclusion of LD in the definitions of handicapping conditions is a lucid example.

CLASSIFICATION OF PEOPLE

LD is a classification scheme, a product of language. It is helpful to view objects, people, and behaviors in groups in order to think and speak of them more easily. It must be remembered that the creation of such classification schemes is purely arbitrary and based on someone's notion of how things should be. A botanist could classify vegetation as being green or nongreen instead of the current method of classification, but the method of classification should be informative and helpful, not trivial or harmful. Current botanical systems are more helpful than green and nongreen. When we classify people's disabilities, it is important to remember the arbitrariness of such systems. Thomas Szasz says:

> The *names*, and hence the *values*, we give to...disabilities—depend on the rules of the system of classification that we use.... Since all systems of classification are made by people, it is necessary to be aware of who has made the rules and for what purpose. If this precaution is not taken, there is the risk of being unaware of the precise rules, or worse, of mistaking the product of classification for "naturally occurring" facts or things.[3]

That is what has occurred in much of the LD literature. A vast number of apparent symptoms were reclassified as a disability, which is frequently called the hidden disability. That name was used to imply that the disability is real but has been overlooked. In fact, it is so hidden that every theory of LD has failed to produce substantial evidence of the reality of LD. Despite that, virtually no one is calling for a decertification of LD as a handicapping condition. Instead some are calling for a return of those students to regular classes with concomitant changes in structure and instructional practices while others are merely calling for a reformulation of the definition. The decisions regarding special education are made by teams. In Pennsylvania those teams are called multidisciplinary teams (MDTs). In other states that can have a host of other names including student assessment teams (SATs). Regardless of the name, the makeup and function of the teams are nearly identical.

THE ROLE OF SPECIAL
EDUCATION TEAMS

The role of the special education team is that of arbiter. It is the team's job to determine to what extent a student is suffering from a perceived handicap. The names we apply to students reflect our current values and arbitrary notions about children. The names depend upon the current system of classification. It has been suggested that we are "allowed to redefine or rename [categories of special education] anytime we get an official quorum to agree."[4] For example, in forty-seven of the fifty states, a student is not mentally retarded unless she has an IQ of less than 70, but in Pennsylvania the current classification system only requires an IQ less than 80. Thus, Pennsylvania has a far larger percentage of mentally retarded youngsters in the school population than nearly any other state.

There can be little doubt of the purposes of involving a multidisciplinary team in the evaluation process. It was to circumvent unilateral decisionmaking and the making of important decisions by individuals. School psychologists were often called the gatekeepers of special education, and it was in response to that view that a multidisciplinary approach was incorporated into the law.

Of course, the ideal of a team making a decision raises several important questions. What is the team supposed to accomplish? How is it to function? Who is to be included on the team? What is each member's role in the process? How are decisions to be reached? Is mere attendance participation? Do certain team members have more power or prestige than other members?

SCREENING FOR SPECIAL EDUCATION

The first step in the trip to special education is the screening process. Usually group achievement and ability tests are used along with teacher reports and observations to determine the need for referral. Once a child is referred for evaluation, he or she will likely be found eligible for special education.[5] Perhaps the most compelling reason for this phenomenon is the ambiguous nature of the special education terms. LD is the primary offender. In fact, when criteria for LD were applied to 248 children from regular classrooms, 85 percent of the students met one or more of the criteria for inclusion in LD services.[6] Thus, it seems likely that unless a building principal or other administrator holds beliefs that run counter to the current thinking in removal of students, special class placement will occur when a teacher is frustrated enough to make a referral for evaluation.

The need for prereferral intervention is obvious in avoiding incorrect identification and placement in special education. Prereferral intervention is usually a systematic attempt by special education teachers and school administrators to help regular education teachers before the implementation of formal evaluation procedures required by law.[7] It is a way of helping children before they get thrown into the special education maze.

SQUANDERING OUR RESOURCES

America has always been a place to squander resources. In the early days, settlers thought nothing of cutting down trees. There were always more. The same is true about how we used our other resources, like water, oil, natural gas, copper, iron ore, bauxite, and on and on. Much the same can be said of how we squander our children.

Ginsberg argues that some implicit assumptions concerning education guide much of what we do in education and that those faulty assumptions lead to difficulties in schools. The assumptions are

1. The child is a passive learner.
2. Education is primarily reading and listening.
3. Children can be grouped and taught roughly the same things at the same time.

4. Learning is facilitated by silence and spontaneous conversation disrupts intellectual activity. If children were allowed to talk the result would be chaos.[8]

Basing education on faulty assumptions about children can do much to damage the children who are most at-risk in school. Providing alternatives to special education youngsters when those alternatives are more of the same is of little benefit.

Let's look again at letter and word reversals. A child who confuses b and d is considered by some to be at-risk. Yet, there are twenty-four other letters of the alphabet that the child does not confuse. Identifying twenty-four letters is never considered as good visual discrimination, yet confusing two letters is considered as evidence of poor visual discrimination.

I believe that children can learn and learn easily and if they are properly motivated and if the right methods are employed. We cannot leave motivation and learning to chance.

NOTES

1. Terman, L. M., & Merrill, M. A. (1973). *Stanford-Binet intelligence scale*. Boston: Houghton Mifflin, p. 98.

2. U. S. Office of Education. Education of handicapped children: Implementation of part b of the education of handicapped act. *Federal Register*, 42(163), August 23, 1977. sec. 612,5(b).

3. Szasz, T. S. (1961). *The myth of mental illness*. New York: Hoeber-Harper, p. 43.

4. Blatt, B. (1985). The implications of the language of mental retardation for LD. *Journal of Learning Disabilities*, 18, p. 625.

5. Ysseldyke, J. E., Algozzine, B., Regan, R., & McCue, M. (1981). The influence of test scores and naturally occurring pupil characteristics on psychoeducational decision making with children. *Journal of School Psychology*, 19, 167-177.

6. Ysseldyke, J. E., Algozzine, B., & Epps, S. (1983). A logical and empirical analysis of current practice in classifying students as handicapped. *Exceptional Children*, 50, 160-166.

7. Pugach, M. C., & Johnson, L. J. (1989). Prereferral interventions: Progress, problems, and challenges. *Exceptional Children*, 56(3), 217-226.

8. Ginsberg, H. (1972). *The myth of the deprived child*. Englewood Cliffs, NJ: Prentice-Hall, p. 218-220.

17

Getting Kids to Join
the Right Club

I would never join a club that would have me as a member.
Groucho Marx

Frank Smith in *Insult to Intelligence*, says that how people view themselves has a lot to do with their performance. If they can do something easily, they see themselves as that type of person. If they cannot do something easily, they see themselves as *not* being that type of person.[1] Smith says it is just like joining a club. Based on what children think they have learned about themselves, they exclude themselves from certain clubs, such as the Reading Club. Instead, they join other clubs, such as the I-Can't-Read Club and cease seeing themselves as the kind of person who can read.

The consequences of such self-views are enormous. Children don't learn what they don't understand, what they are not interested in, or what they don't see people like themselves learning. When they learn they cannot do something, they simultaneously learn what they think about not being able to do it. When children have learned that they cannot read, they join the I-Can't-Read Club. Once a child has joined that club, he no longer sees himself as a reader or tries to learn to read. That is not the type of person he is. To teach a child to read once he has joined the I-Can't-Read Club, requires unlearning as well as learning.

The most important thing you can do as a parent is to keep your children from ever joining the I-Can't-Read Club, the I-Can't-Sit-Still-Club, the I-Don't-Like-Math Club, or any of the other I-Don't or I-Can't Clubs. This chapter deals with a list of actions that you can take to keep your child from enrolling in those clubs. The next chapter deals with getting your child disassociated with those clubs quickly if he has already joined any of them.

WHAT TO DO

As a parent you may be reading this book for one of two reasons—either to keep your children from ever being labeled or to get some help for a child who is already having problems. As a teacher, you may be reading this book to help the children put in your charge. The advice is written to parents but can easily be interpreted for teachers.   Some advice involves preventing problems from occurring, other advice concerns what to do if learning problems have begun to appear or are in full bloom.

1.   First and foremost, whether your child has started school, **you must take charge of your child's education**. Your primary role as a parent is to ensure that your child or children grow up to be responsible, happy adults. In our current society, parents or circumstances are constantly being blamed for the child's failures. It used to be that if a child misbehaved, it was her parents' responsibility to correct the misbehavior. Spare the rod and spoil the child. But no more. Since Freud's time, parents and upbringing are seen as the causes of childhood and eventually adult problems. The bookstores are full of books about how to be a parent as if it is some secret art. Parents have become afraid to control their children's behavior. They do not want to harm them psychologically by being overly controlling, but allowing children to get away with things brands the parents as permissive. There is no way out. If you are going to be blamed for your child's shortcomings either way, step forward and accept the responsibility of child rearing, especially regarding your child's education. Take charge. Don't leave it up to the schools.

Many parents actively teach their children to fish, to wash dishes, to play baseball, to sing, to play chess, to water ski, and to do hundreds of other things that the parents enjoy or think are important. Those same parents will tell you how important a good education is today, yet they may never become involved in their children's education.   They may never teach reading, writing, and arithmetic to their children; they may never check homework; they probably will never attend a parent-teacher conference or go to an open house at school. They believe that it is the school's responsibility to educate their children. After all, isn't that why they pay taxes? They may spend years taking children to Little League games and playing catch, taking them to baton lessons or piano lessons.   They may collect baseball cards together, go hunting and fishing, or teach them to bake, but they may never once discuss school and the value of getting good grades.

Even though I have spent all of my working years in public education, let me warn you—the media reports are correct. Public education is doing a miserable job of educating our children. Interestingly, one of the great paradoxes regarding the terrible state of affairs in public education is people believe that, as a whole, public education is failing. They also believe that the particular school or schools their children attend are doing a good job.[2] The problem with that type of thinking is obvious. How do you get people to insist on educational change when they believe that their children's school is the exception? The answer is that you cannot unless you can convince them that their school is among those doing poor jobs. If your child is already in school and is having difficulty, remember the school's primary concern is not to make sure your child learns to read or cipher. Its primary responsibility is to keep itself in business. Teachers who genuinely care burn out quickly. Schools are more interested in protecting themselves, in filling out the forms, in giving the tests, in following the schedule, in getting funds, than in making sure children learn. Teachers are taught in undergraduate schools that they are not the experts; that they should follow the curriculum of the textbooks. Most teachers and administrators are concerned about children, but they are virtual captives of a bureaucracy run amok. Most of the employees of public education genuinely believe they are doing the right things. They, too, believe that the problems are in other schools or other classrooms. They believe their school, and specifically their class, is doing its job.

Be forewarned, regardless of how good a job you believe your child's school or teacher is doing, do not allow them to be responsible for your child's education, especially if your son or daughter is having difficulty. Ultimately, teachers are responsible to school boards who operate under the auspices of the state. There is little room for experimentation to find ways of teaching a child who is have difficulty. In the final analysis, you must retain the responsibility for your child's education, for only then can you be sure that what is happening is correct. That one premise is the foundation on which all of the rest of the recommendations in this chapter are based. **You are responsible for your child's education.** If he or she is having difficulty, do not under any circumstances rely on the school to pull your child out. The longer you wait for the schools to do their jobs, the further behind your child will get. Take charge and decide for yourself what is needed.

2. Once you believe that you must ultimately call the shots, the rest gets easier. The second thing you must do is **to make sure that you believe in your child's inherent capacity to learn**. All children are lovable and capable. You must believe in that capacity to learn. Your child, regardless of his age, was not raised in a vacuum. He has learned many things. Whether you believe the things he has learned are trivial or not, he has learned them. It has been estimated that 60 percent of everything a person will learn in a lifetime is learned before five years of age. Take an inventory of what your child has learned. Can he or she tie shoes, cut meat, pour a glass of juice, operate the microwave, play Nintendo, hit a baseball, swim, ride a bike, paint, sew, speak a second language? I am sure that you can create quite a list of accomplishments.

Once you have seen the diversity and complexity of what your child has learned probably by three or four years of age, you will recognize the inherent capacity of children to learn and in particular in the capacity of your child to learn. If your child is older than three or four, can he or she hit a baseball, operate the VCR, cook, mow the lawn, drive a tractor, take care of a pet? Children's capacity to learn and do things is virtually endless. A child's brain is programmed to learn easily and completely. Look at the evidence of children's capacity to learn; it is all around us. Children are born to learn; it is part of their genetic makeup.

Remember, reading is as easily learned as most of those other things your child has already learned. Many times, an older sibling can teach a five- or six-year-old child to read. How difficult can it be to teach a child to read if another child can do it? Don't believe you need experts with college degrees to teach reading. Don't treat school work as hand's off for parents. If you and your child get into fights, then get a friend, a neighbor, a grandparent, or hire a tutor, but get someone to teach your child to read.

3. **Develop a philosophy of learning based on the belief of a child's innate capacity to learn**. My philosophy of education is a simple three part statement. First, all children are lovable and capable; second, do nothing to harm them while educating them;

and third, let each child become all that child is capable of becoming. That philosophy has helped guide me in my many years in education. I use the three components as a checklist for all that I do. When confronted with a situation, I ask: Am I seeing the child as capable?, Will what I propose harm this child in any way?, and Will this allow the child to become all he is capable of becoming? You, too, should adopt this or a similar philosophy.

4. **Dismiss LD theory.** LD is only a theory and has yet to be proven. If it were helping kids to pigeonhole them, I would be quiet, but children are being irreparably harmed. Regardless of what experts tell you in general about LD, about letter reversals, perception problems, attention deficits, and the like, get them to talk specifically about you child's problems. If they never get specific, then you can be sure that they do not know what they are talking about. Keep asking them two questions over and over: Under what circumstances? and To what degree? For example, if someone says your son or daughter has a visual perception problem, ask under what circumstances? Only when reading? Can the child pick things up? Can the child walk through a doorway without walking into the wall? Is it only with two dimensional activities on paper? Can you get the child to recognize shapes on a paper? Can the child identify one word? If he can identify even one word, is it fair to categorize him as a student who has visual perception problems? It doesn't matter what he scored on a test if he can read one word. If he can read even one word, he can be taught to read two words, and if two words, he can be taught to read three words and so on. Divide and conquer.

Your job should be to examine the evidence that the pros have. Check it out very carefully. There may be an occasional school-aged child with average intelligence who cannot read even one word. If so, I would be willing to say that child may never be able to learn to read. However, unless the experts can convince you that it is not a condition that comes and goes, unless they can convince you that the condition is permanent and pervasive, do not accept their explanations. Make them get specific. Make them answer the questions Under what circumstances? and To what degree?

5. **Never allow anyone to label your child with a harmful label**. Disabled, disturbed, retarded are not only labels they are also condemnations. The only reason for such a label is to remove a child from a regular education classroom and place her

in a special education classroom "for her own good." Such labels and placements do not help children, they do them harm. Do not allow such labels to be pinned on your child unless an expert can convince you in concrete and specific ways. Read *The Magic Feather*[3] by Lori and Bill Granger who, at first, trusted the school's experts. *The Magic Feather* tells the story of the Grangers' son who had difficulty learning when he was young. Despite the promises the parents received from educators, even in private schools, once tests were administered and scores reported, they followed the boy wherever he went. The Grangers deferred to the experts and were eventually sorry.

The only exception I would make is if your child has a demonstrable medical problem—for example, a hearing impairment—you might consider allowing your child to be labeled to get proper services. Even then, you should ask if the label will make any difference in the manner in which your child will be taught. For example, once your child gets a hearing aid, will there be other differences in her instruction? If not, do not accept the label. Labels restrict regardless of intent.

Do not fall into the trap of looking for a less noxious label. Some people with physical handicaps want to be called physically challenged. Public Law 99-457 changed the preferred term from handicapped to disabled. PL 94-142 was called The Education of All Handicapped Children Act Part B (EHAB) while the revision is called Individuals with Disabilities Act (IDEA). The intent is admirable, but a label is still a label. Treating people as a group, any group, demeans and trivializes. Even if your child cannot read, do math, or sit still, he is still a child. An inability to read should not characterize his worth. If he cannot read, teach him to read. If he cannot do math, teach him math. Do not allow anyone to label him as disabled for the convenience of the schools. A self-fulfilling prophecy will result.

A referral to a psychologist for evaluation is like a challenge to find something wrong. If enough tests are given, eventually someone will find something wrong. Once something is found to be wrong, regardless of how insignificant, the child will be labeled. Once a label has been applied it is like a life sentence. Even if your child overcomes those difficulties, she will always carry the effects of the label with her. Family and friends will always remember that she was in special education. Avoid the label, don't allow the evaluation.

6. If you or the school suspects a learning problem, **never let the school's experts diagnose the problem regardless of the promises you receive**. The school's experts work for the school. They will eventually make decisions based on who is paying their salary. One study found that the best predictor of who would be enrolled in special education was whether a referral to a school psychologist was made.[4] In plain English, children who were referred to be tested for special education usually ended up in special education. Look as the example of Josh I mentioned in chapter 7. Josh was labeled as LD based on one screening test even though he did not qualify for several years. Someone finally caved in to pressure "for the good of the student" and labeled Josh instead of getting the teachers to teach Josh.

Another study reported that accuracy in placements by school psychologists was 66.9 percent.[5] What if your child is in the other one third? If you still have doubts about not allowing school experts to test your child, read Part One of *The Magic Feather*.[6] The Grangers child was seemingly permanently labeled despite the fact that much of the labeling did not help their son. The Grangers even sought the advice of experts outside the schools and got burned. The scores from the experts outside the schools were incorrect. They may even have been intentionally incorrect since the errors were brought to the attention of the testers and were still not corrected.

I know it may be hard for you to reject the services of the local schools when they claim they are only looking out for your child's best interests, but believe me. Once scores have been applied to your child, her worth as a student will be reduced to those scores. I told you of a parent who could not get a psychologist to remove a report that was obviously wrong six years after the testing. Do not trust the school's experts. They are fearful of culpability and lawsuits and ultimately act in their own best interests. Even if they believe that a child is not best served in an LD class, if the student meets the minimum requirements for enrollment, he is almost always enrolled. Educators are afraid not to make those placements.

7. **Set the stage for good school experiences by providing a healthy early education**. Many people have written extensively on the benefits of early experiences. The writing can be summed up with, "As ye sow, so shall ye reap." Young children's experiences shape their futures. A child who is surrounded by love and

acceptance is less likely to have learning problems than a child without. A child born into a nurturing loving family will grow in countless ways. While you child is an infant, cooing, rocking, cuddling, trying to make your baby laugh are the right things to do. Most parents instinctively know how to be parents. Don't listen to the experts or the people next door. Children do not need to be pushed to learn. The best learning takes place in a safe environment where children are willing to take chances.

8. **Make it a habit to read to your child daily**. Even if your child is eleven or twelve years of age, a bedtime story is good for him. Twenty minutes of reading before falling asleep gives you a time to be with your child in a positive atmosphere. When experts talk of quality time, reading fills the bill. It is important that what you read are good stories written by real authors. The stories can be novels or short stories, but they must be rich with plot, narrative, character development and interest. Nearly every library and bookstore has books that list good stories for children, but don't be afraid to read some classics to your child. Adventures like *Moby Dick, Shane, Huckleberry Finn, Anne of Green Gables*, can be read and enjoyed for weeks at a time making bedtime something to look forward to.

Being read to is an experience no child should be without. A child who is read to regularly will be a better reader than a child who hears no stories. It is never too early or too late to start reading to your child on a daily basis. Take him or her to the library and to the bookstores. Buy books; show an interest in them. Read yourself. Turn off the television.

9. **Do not push your child to read**. Children's minds are programmed to learn. They learn quickly and easily when properly motivated, when the time is right. If you don't believe me, think how easily they pick up certain curse words that you or others have uttered in anger. Their learning is often thorough and complete with one exposure. If learning is free of risk, they will not join the I-Can't Club. We put them at-risk for failure with our insistence. Most research points to the concept of when in doubt, hesitate. Of course, there are many children who learn to read before going to school or while in kindergarten, but learning to read is not a race. The first to read is not somehow better or brighter. Reading is a lifelong activity. It should be undertaken when the time is right. Under certain circumstances, some

children read early. The circumstances generally associated with early reading include coming from homes where education is valued, having educated mothers, watching little television, having parents who read, adults who take children places, smaller families, first born or being taught by an older sibling, having chores, dressing independently.[7] Because some children read early does not mean that all children should read early. In fact, here is what some experts say:

> Overanxious adults who apply pressures for early reading, along with pressures of keeping up with classmates, may cause many so-called reading or learning disabilities. Parents and teachers who care, who respond warmly and consistently, who thus create an environment conducive to reading and support children's efforts, greatly facilitate children's learning to read. Motivation of this kind evidently does more for children's reading than exerting undue pressure to achieve or conducting special early school or training programs.... Reading difficulties arising simply from pressured use of immature perceptual processes are often called "disabilities." Yet they may decrease or disappear completely when perceptual abilities improve, usually after the third grade.... For normal and gifted children, little is gained from these early training programs. With perceptual integration and maturation, most children have little difficulty with reading.[8]

The path most parents should take is obvious. Some children will learn to read almost spontaneously. Most will not. Even in the same families, some will learn early, some will not. Providing a supportive, safe environment with opportunities rather than pressures is most important. Some children may be eight or ten years of age before they are perceptually mature enough to tackle reading activities. Unfortunately, with our current philosophy of catching them early, younger and younger children are being captured by labels and condemned to lives of school failure.

10. **If you are unsure of whether to start your child to school, then don't send him or her.** Parents' instincts, often the mother's, should be trusted. The book I just quoted from is entitled *School Can Wait*. Another book that advocates keeping children out until ready is entitled *Don't Push Your Preschooler*.

The premise is simple. If you are not absolutely sure about sending your child to school, keep him or her home. I have talked to dozens of parents who have had questions about whether they should allow their children to start kindergarten or wait for another year. My advice is always the same: When in doubt, keep them out. Some of the parents decided to keep their children out of school for an extra year; some decided to send them. I have never spoken to a parent who was sorry his or her child was kept out an extra year, but I have spoken to several who were sorry they allowed them to go. I realize that personal accounts do not constitute evidence, but the evidence is strongly suggestive that there is no lasting benefit to early instruction but that there may be lasting harm. Do not experiment with your children. Keep them home until you feel sure that they will be successful in school.

11. **Forget readiness activities**. The world is full of people out to make a buck. It's the American way, and I am usually in favor of it, but don't fall prey to people who want to make a buck by promoting your child's lack of preparation. So-called readiness activities, workbooks, and the like that can be purchased at nearly any discount or grocery store have little practical value and may turn children off to education. Filling in blanks and circling pictures may seem like the kinds of things children should be doing to learn to read, but most do not enjoy it. The few who seem to enjoy it, I am convinced, are really more concerned with approval from the adults in their lives. If mom and dad lavish praise and attention on a child for doing seventeen pages of drawing circles around fish and monkeys, then the child will do it for the praise. How much better it would be if the parents were actively engaged in reading to their children.

Imagine life before the modern electronic age. What did parents do for children then? If you can answer that question, you can probably determine what are good readiness activities. Taking children places, playing games with them, telling them stories, allowing them to interact with everyday life, reading to them, letting them follow along as you read, stopping to answer their questions about the words, pointing out letters and sounds, those are the things which constitute readiness activities. Keep away from workbooks and drudgery.

12. Young children delight in sounds and words. They are naturally curious about language and words. **Playing rhyming and alliteration games with them will help them develop a healthy sense of language and prepare them for reading**. While riding in the car, getting dressed, taking a bath, eating supper, make up rhymes for objects you encounter, such as rabbit, habit, grab it. Car, bar, far, tar. Also, use alliteration like Fat Frank is funny.   Little children love to play with words.   The more comfortable they are with words, the more likely they will be to learn to read easily.

13. **Be patient**. Besides love, children need time and space to grow. Growing up is not a race with the neighbors' kids. Just because a child walks and talks early or is potty trained before your child does not mean anything. The race does not always go to the swift. A healthy self-image is far more important. I have known people who have frustrated their children and themselves by trying to hurry mother nature. Preschools are now introducing kindergarten work. Kindergartens are requiring first grade work. Many have become full-day programs. The bookstores are awash with books about teaching your young children reading, math, and science. Many parents are sending their children to swimming lessons at six months. They are getting tap dance lessons, violin lessons, karate lessons before they are four. Children are required to watch "Sesame Street" and "Electric Company." Parents are buying computers for preschoolers so they can be exposed to the wave of the future. Don't fall victim to the big push. Growing up takes time, and what is the hurry to become an adult anyway? Its not that great. A calf can stand and walk in minutes; a baby takes a year. A calf will reach adulthood in three years, a human in 18 years. Which one is better off in the long run?

14. **Don't fall victim to the media hype about precocious youth**. Certainly some children have tremendous abilities. Some of them do graduate from M.I.T. at twelve years of age, but the Doogie Howser syndrome is not all that wonderful.   Many precocious youth have problems we do not hear about. If you had chosen a life for yourself, would it have been to attend college when everyone else was playing soccer and trading baseball cards? Would you really want to sing the national anthem at a baseball game when you were five? Would you want to attend a

private school away from home before you were out of Little League? Media love to glamorize such tales of youthful accomplishment. I am glad that I was merely normal and not a Doogie Howser.

15. Children imitate what others do. **If you truly want your child to read, then read yourself.** If you watch TV from "Good Morning America" to the eleven o'clock news and everything in between, then your child will, too. If you read and enjoy books and share that enjoyment with your children, they will learn to enjoy reading, too. If school is important, go to the open house, meet the teacher, stop in to the school once in a while. Not all teachers discourage parents who come to school. In fact, most primary teachers welcome the chance to discuss what is going on in their rooms. They don't see parents as a threat.

NOTES

1. Smith, F. (1986). *Insult to intelligence*. New York: Arbor House.

2. Finn, C. (1991). *We must take charge: Our schools and our future*. New York: Free Press.

3. Granger, L., & Granger, B. (1986). *The magic feather*. New York: E. P. Dutton.

4. Ysseldyke, J. E., Algozzine, B., & Epps, S. (1983). A logical and empirical analysis of current practice in classifying students as handicapped. *Exceptional Children*, 50, 160-166.

5. Ward, S. B., Ward, T. J., Jr., & Clark III, H. T. (1991). Classification congruence among school psychologists and its relationship to type of referral question and professional experience. *Journal of School Psychology*, 29, 89-108.

6. Granger, L., & Granger, B. (1986). *The magic feather*. New York: E. P. Dutton.

7. Moore, R. S., Moore, D. N., et al. (1979). *School can wait*. Provo, UT: Brigham Young Press.

8. Ibid., p. 105-6.

18

When Your Child Has Already Joined a Club

There are no hopeless situations; there are only men
who have grown hopeless about them.
Author unknown

Most of the suggestions in the previous chapter have to do with preschool or young children, but what of children who are already in school and may already be labeled as LD or who have already become failures at reading? What should you do?

1. **Never get discouraged**. I know it is easy to get discouraged in nearly everything we do, but when it comes to your child's education, you must not give up. Whatever it takes is a motto that many sports teams have adopted. You should adopt it also.

2. **Recognize your child's failure at reading or any other academic activity as temporary**. I have never seen a child with an IQ above 50 who could not read. If your child can identify even one word, such as his name, or McDonald's or Sears, he can read. It's that simple. Reading involves unraveling a code. If your child has the ability to decode once, he can do it again. Once it is clearly established that your child has the physical equipment to recognize print and understand it, (such as recognizing his own name) it should be a dead issue. Your child can recognize a word. If he can recognize one word, he can recognize two. The focus should shift to enhancing the code-breaking ability. It then becomes only a matter of time before a third, a fourth, a fifth code, and so on can be tackled. Poor reading truly becomes a temporary condition.

3. **Find the right teacher**. If you child happens to be in with a malicious malcontent, get him out immediately. If you child is in with a lazy do-nothing, get him out. Do not let your child suffer from a teacher who belittles, bullies, or ignores. It is your right as a citizen to get the kind of education that is being paid for. Insist upon it. In nearly every school district, there are certain teachers who are more understanding and helpful than others. See that your child gets those teachers. Most principals, if given the right reasons, will place children with certain teachers. Find out who the best, most compassionate teachers are, and see that your child gets them.

If there are no compassionate teachers in a particular building, insist on a transfer. If there are no other buildings in the district, or if the district refuses, consider enrollment in a private school. I realize that you are paying taxes for public education, but when your child's future is involved, it is no time to stand on principle. Getting your child into a healthy environment is paramount. Fight the school board, but don't use your child as a weapon. In the unfortunate circumstance that you live in an area in which you can find no nurturing teacher even in a private school, teach your child yourself. Keep him home. Do not subject a young child to bullies or malcontents. Once his reading ability is firmly established, you can re-enroll him in a public school.

4. If your child is in with a good teacher—or at least with a teacher who will do no harm—and is having academic difficulties, **get a tutor for help outside of school**. Sometimes parents are able to fill the function of tutor, but beware. If there are conflicts, do not continue instructing your own child. It is more important to get someone who will help her than to allow your ego to get in the way. Parents can find it difficult to instruct their own children because of the emotional attachment and vested interest. It is far better to get a neighbor, an aunt, a grandmother, or hire a tutor than it is to put further stress on a child who probably feels like a failure anyhow. Hiring a tutor for help with homework and to instruct in reading does not mean you are a poor parent. If people suggest something like that, they just are not tuned in to the emotional stress under which a child who is having difficulty in school can put on the entire family. Seek outside help. Ignore the backbiters.

If you do hire a tutor, be sure that the tutor is a positive, supporting person. Getting help from a demanding or demeaning person will do no good. You must find someone who is gentle and kind but who understands enough schooling to be helpful. A college education can sometimes be a detriment, so do not look only for certified teachers. Sometimes people who have had no formal training are better tutors. Caring and compassion are needed more than knowledge of reading or math. A next-door neighbor or a relative to whom your child seems to be drawn is a far better choice than a certified teacher who tries to teach reading using a textbook.

Be sure that you have clearly established ground rules and that the tutor understands his or her role. Tutoring can be of two main types—direct instruction to learn a skill or support for class work with which the student is having trouble. If you are not satisfied with the type of reading instruction your child has been receiving, it certainly will not help to get him tutored with the materials that you think are no good. Instead, look for a tutor who will teach reading using newspapers, books, and magazines rather than reading series. Look for someone who has taught his or her own child to read in a relaxed fashion. A person who likes to read and takes great pleasure in reading can instill that same love in a child who has difficulty reading and has enrolled in the I-Can't-Read Club. Marva Collins is just such a person. She got inner city dropouts to start reading Shakespeare and other classics because of her love for them. People like Marva Collins are not hard to find. They spend their time reading and want others to be able to read.

A good reading tutor will read to your child and allow him to follow along. A good tutor will teach phonics and word attack skills. A child who is surrounded with written language and enjoys having someone read to him, a child who sees others around him enjoying reading, will learn to read without having to be pushed or prodded. I am not going to give specific details for I do not believe that is necessary or productive. An adult who is not threatening and who enjoys reading almost intuitively knows what to do to get a child hooked on reading. There are many books on how to teach reading at home. Many of them are written by people who are no more expert at teaching reading than the woman or man next door who helped his or her own children. Reading milk cartons and cereal boxes at breakfast and road signs and billboards in the car are the types of learning that show that parents are interested. Making sure it does not come from coercion but from genuine interest usually means it is good reading instruction.

5. **Forget the praise.** Regardless of what you have heard about lavish amounts of praise, it is a manipulative and deceitful thing to do, and children see through it anyhow. A condescending "Very good!" every few seconds, or "Nice job!" or "You've worked hard, today!" are intended to trick a child into doing what he would not normally do. Can you imagine a mother standing over a ten year old while he is eating an ice cream sundae and telling him, "Nice job! You were a good boy to eat all of your ice cream." Of course not. The ice cream is reward enough. Imagine standing over the same child and forcing him to eat whale blubber, monkey's brains, or some other delicacy from another part of the world. Will the oral praise get him to enjoy them? No, it won't, and neither will interjecting a "Very, very good!" make you son or daughter a better reader or make him or her enjoy reading. Good books, good stories, rich narratives, plot development are all that is needed. Children don't have to be praised to watch *Batman Returns*. Why should they have to be praised to read an Edgar Allen Poe short story? Poe is reward enough.

6. **When you start accepting responsibility for your child's education, be prepared for resistance**. Schools are not set up for parents to ensure that their children are getting a proper education. They are set up for smooth, efficient operation. Teachers and principals sometimes do not want to be questioned by parents or to justify what they do to parents. It is still the parents' right and responsibility to ensure that what is being taught and how it is being taught is in you child's best interests. Don't back away from that responsibility just because the schools may balk. Whenever you approach the schools to have a meeting, take along a notebook and summarize what occurred. Keep all correspondence. Recount phone conversations in your notebook. At some point you may find yourself in a due process hearing or in a meeting with the school superintendent. Keeping track of your meetings with teachers and principals may be of benefit.

Just a word about due process hearings. Do not back down just because the district threatens to hold a hearing. The due process hearings I have attended or read transcripts from have always been impartial and have found in favor of the right side.

You may get involved in a hearing if you want your child who is already identified to be taken out of special education classes. You may also find yourself in a due process hearing if you refuse to allow the school district to test your child. Regardless, never allow them to test.

Should you be in a due process hearing, sometimes it is advisable to have an attorney. I have seen several parents present evidence on their own who have done a commendable job, but hearings are getting far more formal. School districts are bringing their solicitors and are objecting to the types of evidence being entered and the procedures being employed. If you are not confident in those proceedings, hire an attorney. If you win, you can recover attorneys' fees from the district in court.

If you have a meeting with a psychologist or are in a hearing, ask that every vague term be explained in layperson's terms. Keep asking until you understand. Your next question should then be, In all cases? Rarely, if ever is there an every case scenario. Ask how your child came to be included. Is it a 100 percent chance? What skill deficits have caused him to be referred or labeled? Can you teach them to him? For example, if your child cannot tell b from d, can he be taught it? Another good question, What if I gave him one million dollars? Could he do it then?

Tell the teacher that you want any reasons for referring your child in writing, in behavioral terms. Teachers are good at saying that "Johnny can't sit still." Find out what that really means. Did he get out of his seat once in an hour, twice, half a dozen times? If the teacher says "Johnny has difficulty with math." What does that mean? Can he add, subtract, single digits, double digits? Can he borrow and carry? Get the teacher to quantify, then ask what the teacher did to help or to stop the behavior. Did the teacher insist that he sit down and not get up? What happened then? Did the teacher directly instruct Johnny in addition of single digits? What happened? Ask if you can teach him those skills at home. Don't be put off by teachers who assure you that it is their job to teach. Insist that you or a tutor help if he is having difficulty.

7. **If your child has already been diagnosed and placed in an LD program, or if he is having difficulty in school, get counseling for him**. Be careful, however. The wrong kind of counseling is worse than no counseling. Look for a counselor who

believes in individual abilities and overcoming temporary set backs. Look for a counselor who does not believe strongly in testing and disabilities. A counselor who does not believe in limits is what you want. Goal setting and working toward those goals are what is called for. A child who is having difficulty in school needs someone to assure her that it is the school's system and not the child that is at fault. The counselor should work hand in hand with any tutor you have hired. The counselor you select need not be a professional counselor. You may even select the tutor to be a counselor, for formal counseling is not necessary as much as some good advice from a caring, inspiring adult. Let the tutor read this book. Make sure the tutor agrees with what I have to say.

8.   There is one warning I would make about reading problems. **Rule out vision problems**. Occasionally, children with vision problems have difficulty reading. If the left and right eyes do not focus together, reading is almost impossible. Look for an ophthalmologist who specializes in children's vision problems. Many eye doctors are not trained or equipped to deal with the special problems that some children have. They deal exclusively with acuity or diseases. It may be that your child is one of the few with visual problems so severe that interpreting print is nearly impossible. Corrective lenses can be prescribed to rectify many perception problems. Be careful because some ophthalmologists wish to sell you a series of perception tasks rather than emphasize real reading. Insist on real reading.

9.   If reading is a problem, **use a phonics approach to teaching reading, but beware of paralysis by analysis**. Golfers refer to overanalysis of the swing as paralysis by analysis. Once you become too technical, you lose the ability to be free-flowing and smooth. The same is true in reading—overemphasizing sounding out words will lead to the same kind of paralysis. A good presentation of the phonics method is contained in *Why Johnny Can't Read—And What You Can Do About It.*[1] Use it, but don't overemphasize it. And, for heaven's sake, don't buy those phonics workbooks you find in the children's section of the bookstore.

10. **If you or a tutor is to teach reading, avoid pointless and discouraging busywork**. Several scholars have criticized the teaching of reading because it has been reduced to nothing but

busywork. Frank Smith, Bruno Bettelheim, and Benjamin Fine are among the critics. They are concerned about the wasteland of reading series and workbooks, devoid of interest and good language. The stores are written by committees of instructional specialists instead of real authors. Filling in the missing word or letter substitutes for real learning. Do not use those kinds of instructional materials. Use books with real stories. Dr. Seuss knew what children like. The major reading series publishers do not.

11. **Do not fall into the beliefs about innate intelligence**. Some people write off their children because of a score on an intelligence test. Intelligence is not innate and IQ tests do not measure intelligence. (See chapter 6.) Intelligence can be taught and IQ scores can change significantly. Reading achievement is not strongly linked to IQ scores either.

12. Sports psychologists tell athletes to **make your weakness your strength**. Parents can do the same for their children. A child who is weak at spelling can be taught to be good at it and in effect, make that weakness a strength. Practice and effort are needed. If the problem is great, then a great deal of effort is needed, but do not give up because you child is not good at something.

13. If behavior is a problem, **tell your child specifically and directly what to do and not to do**. Put your foot down. Do not let her get away with anything. Insist the school do the same. If necessary, go to school and sit in the room with your child and make her behave until she knows you mean business. Getting out of her seat to sharpen a pencil or get a drink may be perceived by some teacher as attention deficit disorder (ADD). Don't let your child gain a label because she does not follow directions. Everything I have said about LD is also true of ADD. It is a label applied by adults to children who do not measure up. It is an excuse to give medicine instead of discipline. You would not handcuff your child. Do not allow a doctor to apply chemical handcuffs. Give specific directions to your child and insist that she follow them. Do not allow a child who is out of her seat in school to be drugged to control her.

14. **Don't be confused by special education jargon**. Every profession has its own jargon. The purpose of a professional vocabulary is to enhance communication but, in fact, it often obscures communication. As I suggested in point 6, ask about every confusing or vague term. Do not be intimidated by someone else's careless use of letters and phrases to throw you off. Most educators do not know that they are condescending by their use of jargon. When they speak of IEPs, NORAs, MDEs and the like, ask what they mean. If they say a team writes the IEP, ask who is on the team and who did the actual writing. Pin down every generalization.

Ultimately, all children have the capacity to learn far beyond what is expected of them. Unfortunately, to a large extent, adult expectations determine children's level of learning. Unenlightened educators have come to believe that America is delivering faulty merchandise to be educated. The belief is that it is not the school's fault if children don't learn; they were not good material before they got to school. The schools know that attacking the family and the students deflects attention from them. Remember, special education does not help but it has been sold so successfully, that virtually no one sees it for what it is, a vast wasteland of discouraged youth. Not much has changed since. Take charge of your child's education. If he has skill deficits, determine what they are; divide and conquer. Teach him or hire a tutor, but do not sentence him to a wholly negative label. LD simply does not exist. Do not believe that it does exist.

A FINAL WORD

In chapter 1, I asked the following question: If changing beliefs would change children's performance, if LD theory is wrong, would you want to continue to perpetrate such a terrible lie on America's youth? The question is structured in such a way that there can only be one answer unless you are insensitive. Of course, no one wants to keep calling children LD if it is wrong. The question is a trick question because it has two *ifs* in it. Change those *ifs* to *sinces* and you have an entirely different question. *Since* changing beliefs would change children's performance, *since* LD theory is wrong, do you want to continue to perpetrate such as terrible lie on America's youth? The question is now laughable.

If you want to change children's lives for the better, you must believe that LD is a made-up category used to segregate and ultimately harm children. You must also believe that children are immensely capable; that LD is, in fact, a well-intentioned but ill-conceived movement that has run amok; that children are being placed on a disability trajectory toward failure and low self-

esteem; that the consequences of the label are so severe and children are so harmed that we must end this category quickly and forever. Only then will we quit shuffling them down the hall to second-class status. The LD experience treats children as if they are dumb, as if they do not measure up.

Believe in children. Believe in their innate capacities to learn far more than we expect them to learn. They are infinitely more capable than we think. Take the steps to ensure that academics do not fall behind. Proper instruction is the real answer. Don't believe the experts who want to label and segregate. Don't let anyone assign a label that harms you or your children. You are in charge.

NOTE

1. Flesch, R. (1955). *Why Johnny can't read–and what you can do about it*. New York: Harper.

Bibliography

Affleck, J. Q., Madge, S., Adams, A., & Lowenbraun, S. (1988). Integrated classroom versus resource model: Academic viability and effectiveness. *Exceptional Children*, 54(4), 339-348.

Algozzine, B. (1985). Low achiever differentiation: Where's the beef? *Exceptional Children*, 52(1), 72-75.

Algozzine, B., & Ysseldyke, J. E. (1983). Learning disabilities as a subset of school failure: The oversophistication of a concept. *Exceptional Children*, 50(3), 242-246.

Ames, L. B. & Chase, J. A. (1980). *Don't push your preschooler.* New York: Harper & Row.

Armstrong, T. (1987). *In their own way: Discovering and encouraging your child's personal learning style.* New York: St. Martin's Press.

Barsch, R. (1986). A plea for a new direction. *Academic Therapy*, 22(1), 5-10.

Blatt, B. (1985). The implications of the language of mental retardation for LD. *Journal of Learning Disabilities*, 18, 625-626.

Boring, E. G. (1923). Intelligence as the tests test it. *New Republic*, 6, 35-37.

Burkhardt, M. (1981). Introduction. In Flesch, R. *Why Johnny still can't read.* New York: Harper & Row.

Carlberg, C., & Kavale, K. (1980). The efficacy of special versus regular class placement for exceptional children: A meta-analysis. *Journal of Special Education*, 14(3), 295-309.

Chilman, C. S. (1966). *Your child from 6 to 12.* Washington, DC: U.S. Government Printing Office.

Coles, G. (1987). *The learning mystique.* New York: Pantheon.

Epps, S., & Tindal, G. (1987). The effectiveness of differential programming in serving students with mild handicaps: Placement option and instructional programming. In M. C. Wang, M. C. Reynolds, & H. J. Walberg (eds.). *Handbook of special education: Research and practice vol. 1 learner characteristics and adaptive education*. New York: Pergamon.

Epps, S., Ysseldyke, J. E., & McGue, M. (1984). "I know one when I see one": Differentiating LD and non-LD students. *Learning Disability Quarterly*, 7(1), 89-101.

Flesch, R. (1955). *Why Johnny can't read--and what you can do about it*. New York: Harper.

Flesch, R. (1981). *Why Johnny still can't read*. New York: Harper & Row.

Finn, C. (1991). *We must take charge: Our schools and our future*. New York: Free Press.

Fuller, R. (1977). *In search of the IQ correlation: A scientific whodunit*. Stony Brook, NY: Ball-Stick-Bird Publications.

Gartner, A. (1986). Disabling help: Special education at the crossroads. *Exceptional Children*, 53(1), 72-76.

Gearheart, B. R. & Gearheart, C. J. (1989). *Learning disabilities: Educational strategies*. Columbus: Merrill.

Ginsberg, H. (1972). *The myth of the deprived child*. Englewood Cliffs, NJ: Prentice-Hall.

Greene. L. J. (1986). *Kids who underachieve*. New York: Simon & Schuster.

Granger, L. & Granger, B. (1986). *The magic feather*. New York: E. P. Dutton.

Guilford, J. P. (1959). *Personality*. New York: McGraw-Hill.

Hunt, N. (1967). *The world of Nigel Hunt; The diary of a mongoloid youth*. New York: Garrett Publications.

John, K. M., Gutkin, T. B., & Plake, B. S. (1991). Use of modeling to enhance children's interrogative strategies. *Journal of School Psychology*. 29, 81-88.

Johnson, G. O. (1962). Special education for the mentally handicapped-- A paradox. *Exceptional Children*, 29, 62-69.

Kavale, K. A. (1988). The long-term consequences of learning disabilities. In Wang, M. C., Reynolds, M. C., & Walberg, H. J. (Eds.). *Handbook of special education: Research and practice volume 2 mildly handicapped conditions*. New York: Pergamon.

Lair, J. (1985). *I Ain't Much Baby, but I'm All I've Got*. New York: Faucett.

Lerner, J. W. (1971). *Children with learning disabilities: Theories, diagnosis, and teaching strategies*. New York: Houghton Mifflin.

Lewontin, R. C., Ross, S. P. R., & Kamin, L. J. (1984). *Not in our genes: Biology, ideology, and human nature*. New York: Pantheon.

Lippmann, W. (1976). The abuse of tests. In Bloch, N. J. & Dworkin, G. (Eds.) *The IQ Controversy: Critical Readings*. New York: Pantheon Books.

Lippmann, W. (1976). The abuse of tests. In Bloch, N. J. & Dworkin, G. (Eds.) *The IQ Controversy: Critical Readings*. New York: Pantheon Books.

McKnight, R. T. (1982). The learning disability myth in American education. *Journal of Education*, 164(4), 351-359.

Mitchell, R. (1981). *The graves of academe*. Boston: Little, Brown.

Moore, R. S., Moore, D. N., et al. (1979). *School can wait*. Provo, UT: Brigham Young Press.

Moore, R. S. (1977). *Better late than early : A new approach to your child's education*. New York: Reader's Digest Press.

Mosse, H. L. (1982). *You can prevent or correct learning disorders; The complete handbook of children's reading disorders*. New York: Teachers College Press.

Noel, M. M., & Fuller, B. C. (1985). The social policy construction of special education: The impact of state characteristics on identification and integration of handicapped children. *Remedial and Special Education*, 6(3), 27-35.

Orwell, G. (1968). Politics and the english language. In *The collected essays, journalism, and letters of George Orwell. Volume IV in front of your nose 1945-50*. London: Secher & Warburg.

Pugach, M. C., & Johnson, L. J. (1989). Prereferral interventions: Progress, problems, and challenges. *Exceptional Children*, 56(3), 217-226.

Ross, A. O. (1976). *Psychological aspects of learning disabilities & reading disorders*. New York: McGraw-Hill.

Ross, A. O. (1977). *Learning disability the unrealized potential*. New York: McGraw-Hill.

Rothman, E. P. (1972). *The angel inside went sour*. New York: Bantam.

Rourke, B. P. (1989). Coles's learning mystique: The good, the bad, and the irrelevant. *Journal of Learning Disabilities*, 22(5), 274-277.

Sabatino, D. A. (1971). An evaluation of resource rooms for children with LD. *Journal of Learning Disabilities*, 4(2), 27-35.

Schrag, P., & Divoky, D. (1975). *The myth of the hyperactive child*. New York: Dell.

Siegel, J. (1989). Is IQ necessary in the identification of LD? *Journal of Learning Disabilities*, 22(8), 487-492.

Shinn, M. R., Ysseldyke, J. E., Deno, S. L., & Tindal, G. A. (1986). *Journal of Learning Disabilities*, 19(9), 545-552.

Sigmon, S. B. (1989). Reaction to excerpts from The Learning Mystique: A rational appeal for change. Journal of Learning Disabilities, 22(5), 298-327.

Sigmon, S. B. (1990). *Critical voices on special education*. Albany: State University of New York Press.

Smith, F. (1986). *Insult to intelligence*. New York: Arbor House.

Spearman, C. (1904). General intelligence objectively measured and determined. *American Journal of Psychology*, 15, 201-293.

Stainbach, S., & Stainbach, W. (1984). A rationale for the merger of special and regular education. *Exceptional Children*, 51, 475-476.

Stanovich, K. E. (1989). Has the learning disabilities field lost its intelligence? *Journal of Learning Disabilities*, 22(8), 487-492.

Szasz, T. S. (1961). *The myth of mental illness.* New York: Hoeber-Harper.

Terman, L. M. & Merrill, M. A. (1973). *Stanford-Binet intelligence scale.* Boston: Houghton Mifflin.

U. S. Office of Education. (1977). Education of handicapped children: Implementation of part B of the education of handicapped act. *Federal Register*, 42(163), August 23.

Valentine, M. R. (1987). *How to deal with discipline problems in the schools: A practical guide for educators.* Dubuque, IA: Kendall/Hunt.

Wang, M. C., & Baker, E. T. (1985-86). Mainstreaming programs: Designs features and effects. *Journal of Special Education*, 19, 503-525.

Ward, S. B., Ward, T. J., Jr., & Clark III, H. T. (1991). Classification congruence among school psychologists and its relationship to type of referral question and professional experience. *Journal of School Psychology*. 29,89-108.

Whimbey, A. (1975). *Intelligence can be taught.* New York: Dutton.

White, S. H. (1977). Social implications of IQ. In Houts, P. L. (ed.), *The myth of measurability.* New York: Hart Publishing.

Ysseldyke, J. E., Algozzine, B., & Epps, S. (1983). A logical and empirical analysis of current practice in classifying students as handicapped. *Exceptional Children*, 50, 160-166.

Ysseldyke, J. E., Algozzine, B., Regan, R., & McCue, M. (1981). The influence of test scores and naturally occurring pupil characteristics on psychoeducational decision making with children. *Journal of School Psychology*, 19, 167-177.

Ysseldyke, J. E., Algozzine, B., Shinn, M. R., & McGue, M. (1982). Similarities and differences between low achievers and students classified as learning disabled. *Journal of Special Education*, 16, 73-85.

Zelan, K. (1991). *The risks of knowing.* New York: Plenum.

Index

About the Author

THOMAS G. FINLAN is Director of Special Education at the Riverview Inter-mediate Unit in Pennsylvania. He has a Ph.D. in Educational Administration from Pennsylvania State University and has contributed to LD journals as well as a book, *Helping At-Risk Students* (1992).